The Incredibly Biased Beer Guide

Ruth Herman

SIGMA Leisure

Published by Sigma Leisure – an imprint of
Sigma Press, 1 South Oak Lane, Wilmslow, Cheshire SK9 6AR, England.

British Library Cataloguing in Publication Data
A CIP record for this book is available from the British Library.

ISBN: 1-85058-376-5

Typesetting and Design by: Sigma Press, Wilmslow, Cheshire.

Cover photograph: Richard Marshall

Printed by: Manchester Free Press

Acknowledgments
Various brand names used in this book may be trademarks and are used for descriptive purposes only. All illustrations are supplied by the breweries concerned and are copyright protected. The illustration on page 13 is by Joe Gill, and is a sketch of part of his father's Springhead Brewery.

Foreword

Welcome to the *Incredibly Biased Beer Guide* and thank you for parting with your hard earned cash! I do hope that you find this interesting, for the idea behind the book was to introduce people directly to small brewers throughout the UK and to pubs that support those companies.

Although I have been asked to write this introduction in my capacity as Chairman of the Small Independent Brewers Association it is hard for me to divorce my comments from the everyday experiences I have as a brewer who finds all aspects of the trade fascinating, and especially its historic development.

My family ran pubs in South Wales and I remember the great pride taken by them in the beers they served and the service they gave. But, looking back at photographs of those pubs, I see businesses that were neglected by the breweries which owned them. Indeed, the impression that this industry is slowly dying because of misguided investment is strong in my mind. Its continuing attempts to avoid competition and maintain profit centrally prevent real dynamism and this, sadly, despite the very best efforts of many who work in it, ends with the customers losing out.

However, the many and varied pubs in this guide together with the literally hundreds of beers represented show that there is still hope for this once great industry. Regrettably the good pubs are few and far between and the beers brewed by small independents represent less than 1% of beer sold – yet, incredibly, they brew twice as many different beers as the other 99%.

Throughout the 19th century, anybody with two guineas could open a "public" house but for a variety of reasons (mainly that people were getting drunk too often!) the free issue of on-licences was halted in the 1870s. The politicians were aware at the time that this gave breweries who owned pubs a "privileged" position as they effectively could avoid competition. This gave these companies a strong base from which to grow. Ironically, however, it sowed the seeds of their demise for an arrogance developed as new generations forgot the privilege that Parliament had bestowed upon them.

It is because of this that these families became known as the "Beerage" – for their financial power has enabled them to influence legislation at the very highest levels. The 1989 Monopolies & Mergers Commission investigation damned the industry by stating that it worked against the public interest, but the resulting legislation was a diluted hotch-potch which failed to introduce competition as promised: beer prices continue to escalate. We have recently seen this influence in action as the national companies have persuaded the EC to extend the "block exemption". This maintains the tied house system, despite it being contrary to European law. These companies even have the gall to ask the Government to reduce beer duty because sales are going down!

Regrettably, it is you – the customer – who loses out. The other industries that have been able to consistently put up their prices during a recession are banks and insurance companies – for they too enjoy legally-protected positions. And we all love them, don't we! As always, the answer lies in your hands so remember that your purchase has great significance. When you next buy a pint or go to a pub, buy a pint from a truly independent brewer and from a pub which supports these companies.

The Small Independent Brewers Association seeks to represent our members' interests at the very highest levels of Government, but our efforts are always overshadowed by representations on behalf of national and regional brewers determined to maintain their power. The continuing support and encouragement of your local brewers who brew better, cheaper beer and provide greater choice will help create a healthier and more competitive industry.

Cheers and Beers!

David Roberts – Chairman, Small Independent Brewers Association

PREFACE

Why a book about small independent brewers? Well, enough people write about beer. Through the efforts of organisations like the Campaign for Real Ale, beer has become elevated from the humble national drink of the British to an all-absorbing hobby. So again – why should I write a book about these brewers? It's not because they have set up their own little businesses – thousands of people must have done that over the past ten years. It is more because they are a group of people in the British Isles who have taken on the might of large international corporations and been an influence for the better.

What is the definition of a small independent brewer? Quite apart from size, I think it is a question of attitude. Large brewers make beer for profit, to make money for their shareholders, generally as part of a range of connected industries. Small independent brewers also produce their beer for profit, they too need to eat; but they also brew out of pleasure, pride and for a multitude of other reasons. Some of them really did start up to make a small personal protest about the overmighty national brewers. Some of them saw brewing as a way of achieving a life which would offer satisfaction and freedom. Some of them went into the business because they believed their own beer was good enough to share with the rest of the world. Each person's motivation was different, but the end was the same – independence!

So what makes someone give up a secure career or take their precious redundancy package and sink everything into a small brewery? Is it a love of beer, independence or plain foolhardiness? There are as many reasons for becoming a brewer as there are breweries and *The Incredibly Biased Beer Guide* gives some insight into the personalities behind many of the small breweries which have sprung up over the past twenty years. The one common denominator among these brave souls is that they all belong to the Small Independent Brewers Association, the small brewers' trade association. These people are very independent – they brew different beers in different towns all over the British Isles. The breweries are everything from beautifully restored farm buildings overlooking the Devon coast to soulless units on industrial estates. Some operate in brewpubs, some refuse to run pubs at all. They sell their beers all over the country, or will not allow it further than a ten-mile radius of their own premises. They have been everything from headmasters to stage-managers, accountants to secretaries and most occupations in between.

Also included in the book is a list of the brewers' favourite pubs. If you have always wondered where they go to relax or where they would ask someone to take them for a drink, here's a chance to find out. The reasons they have given for their choice are equally personal. The beer must be good – although not necessarily their own – a brewer will not frequent a pub where he or she can't trust the landlord to serve a decent pint. But every pub listed has something special about it, good food, a good atmosphere or a landlord or landlady who is a personality in their own right. All the pubs are worth searching for. They all carry small independent brewers' ales and they have all been recommended by a small independent brewer.

As background to this world of self-confessed eccentrics, dedicated brewers and artists-in-ale, I have included a brief resume of what I have considered amusing bits of brewing history in the British Isles, from the Romans up to the last century, when brewing became very big business. It is not an academic survey, but a collection of bits and pieces that I hope you will find interesting, amusing and useful in conversation over a good pint of independent beer.

The book is indeed 'Incredibly Biased' because it has been written from a purely personal point of view. It is for beer drinkers or pub goers of all levels of enthusiasm and interest. It is a way of seeing just how much effort has gone into the pint of beer that you drink, why there are so many small breweries springing up every year, and why so many of them are so successful. It is also a celebration of a spirit of independence which has not only survived battering from big business and successive governments, but which is also thriving even in these days of recession. The movement had a delicate infancy and now it is reaching maturity and beginning to develop a strong personality of its own. Perhaps we should view this book as only the first volume of its biography. There are many years of adventures to come!

The Small Independent Brewers Association

Quite a few years ago, some far sighted individuals thought that they could revolutionise the British brewing industry, or at least make their own little mark on it. To find out more about this part of the story read about Ringwood brewery and how Peter Austin started up all those years ago. In the meantime it became more and more obvious that these little brewers, in order to have any influence at all over the great and good in government and the media would have to band together to speak with one voice rather than lots of little squeaks.

So The Small Independent Brewers Association was born some eleven years ago. Over the years the Association has grown from a small band of gutsy individuals to an organisation which works on behalf of the small brewers of the country (by small I mean *really* small – not the regional brewers who dominate large tracts of the country with their own pubs and beers). Of course, the aims of the Association are principally to benefit the brewers, but ultimately their success will ensure the survival of these individual businesses which provide so much of the zest of this country's brewing industry. For it is an interesting fact that from a tiny proportion of the capacity of the brewing industry, come around 50% of the different beers available to the British drinker. The small independent brewers popularised the brew pub, brought porter to the public attention and re-introduced mild. All this from a bunch of people living on overdrafts and sometimes producing less than one hundred gallons of beer a week.

The reason for this is of course that they can afford to take chances, be flexible and brew to order. They will sometimes produce a beer for a special occasion or will simply brew one barrel to see if their local pub likes it! Try getting a national brewer to do that! Again some of them do have their own pubs where they can try things out on customers, but more often than not they are dependent on the success of each individual barrel they sell. One duff one and they have lost that pub as a customer.

The Serious Message

You may remember a few years ago something called the Monopolies and Mergers Commission on the Brewing Industry. These clever people, asked by the government to find out what was wrong with the way of selling beer, decided that the large companies had far too much power over the market and therefore they should have some curb to their influence. So the government in their wisdom decreed that no brewer should own more than a certain number of tied houses (pubs which are both owned and therefore supplied exclusively by a particular brewery). They also decreed that each pub should be allowed at least one beer which was of the publican's choosing. 'What a good idea', I hear the beer drinker say. 'And a wonderful way of making sure that small independent brewers have a market for what they make'.

Alas, like so many good ideas, if only the execution had matched up to the intention. What really happened was that the brewers sold their excess pubs off and negotiated contracts with the new owners which would ensure that they still maintained a tight control over the beer that could be sold. Of course the guest ale policy did sometimes work in the small independent brewers' favour. It meant that some pubs do indeed maintain at least one beer pump for an ever changing selection of brews. And of course there is still the genuine free house, a pub owned by a non-brewer who makes their own choice of what beer they will buy, based on public demand and what is most economical for him or her. (This does mean that sometimes the national brewers, desperate to keep their share of the market will offer their beer at extraordinarily low rates, but that's business!) But what is more significant for the small independent brewer (and the local beer drinker) is that this 'hidden ownership' of pubs means that it is sometimes very difficult for a brewer to sell his beer into his local pubs, despite their being 'free houses'. This in turn forces the brewer to distribute his beer all over the country using wholesalers. Wouldn't it be better if the brewer could be sure of selling his beer to his neighbours? So if there is a message in this book, it is this: if you read of a brewery that is nearby to you, but you can't buy their beer in your local, ask the publican why not – it's often not because he doesn't want to, but more likely that he is not allowed to. So, if you like your friendly neighbourhood small independent brewer's beer, make a stand – remember: 'Think local – drink local!'

Ruth Herman

CONTENTS

A Very Biased History of Beer and Pubs

They can't all be wrong!

The Prince Regent is said to have remarked of his countrymen: 'Beef and Beer made us what we are'. The Reverend Sydney Smith said: 'What two ideas are more inseparable than Beer and Britannia? Here's a health to the brewer and God speed the plough'. One economist reckoned that the average household spent more on beer and ale than any other single commodity.

Dr Johnson in the eighteenth century also said: 'There is nothing which has yet been contrived by man, by which so much happiness is produced as by a good tavern or inn'.

All these notable thinkers can't have been wrong – and even today many people would say that it is hard to beat a good pint of English beer as a living reminder of the heritage of the best of Olde Englande.

In the Beginning

If we look back into history it has not always been so. Beer has had a chequered career, and has often been blamed for many of the ills of the past. Even as far back as the first century AD a Greek physician was complaining that a drink similar to one made in Britain 'and often drunk instead of wine produces headaches, is a compound of bad juices and does harm to the muscles.' I hope the physician, Dioscorides, never visited Roman Britain, because he would have been appalled at the number of our earliest ale-houses established in the cities to provide refreshment and rest for travellers.

After the Romans went, the Saxons may have forgotten all about the bath-houses and the central heating, but they recognised the sense of having their own early version of a motorway service station. Many of them set up their wooden huts along the old Roman roads and plied their new trade as ale-house keepers, providing drinks for thirsty travellers. They used what was the first universally recognised inn sign, a long pole which said loud and clear to the passing trade 'Ale on sale here'.

Maybe in those early centuries of English civilisation there would also have been a ready market for the home-brew kit. For in those days, brewing was a family affair at first, with the women of each household brewing for their own family. Fairly soon, however, it was realised that bulk-brewing was probably more sensible and communities started to brew cooperatively.

As we move on through the years, the Church came to dominate the lives of the English rural population and what could be more sensible, since they controlled the festival calendar for the Church to control the brewing process? So the large religious establishments began to exert their influence on the steadily growing brewing industry. They also seemed to have had an influence on the beginnings of the hospitality trade, since they held themselves responsible for providing stopping stations for travellers (within reason).

Package holidays took the form of pilgrimages in the middle ages. ('Take a leisurely stroll along the Pilgrim's Way spending three nights in the modern city of Canterbury where you can enjoy the night life and during the day visit the tomb of the martyred St Thomas à Becket' – they were lucky the printing press had not yet reached the stage where it could print tour brochures!) The mediaeval church, with an eye to the wealthy, said that travellers taking trips could stay in church-provided accommodation. There were also hostels built by religious institutions near to the more popular shrines where you could stay for a couple of days, unless there were some good reason why you could not move on. Payment was at the discretion of the traveller, so that although there was no fixed charge you gave what you could. (Perhaps a little piece of 'Olde England' the hotel business would care to revive today – if the facilities are mediaeval, why not the charging system?)

However, the Church did have some competition very early on, some of which was so attractive that it was proving irresistible for the clerics themselves. Already by the eighth century, one spoil-sport Archbishop of York was issuing orders that priests were forbidden to eat or drink in taverns. In 1175 clerics were forbidden to frequent taverns (unless on their travels) and were forbidden from being present at public drinking bouts.

This was obviously only the start of authority's determination to keep the drinking habits of the English people under control. Two centuries later, enterprising King Edgar invented weights and measures and his own version of the monopolies and mergers commission. He tackled the distribution side of the drinks industry by declaring that there were too many ale-houses and restricting their numbers to one to each village. His contribution to trading standards was far more inventive and is probably the nearest thing the middle ages got to that little line on the pint glass that tells you what you're getting. He ordered that the communal drinking vessels that were popular in those days should be fitted with a row of evenly spaced pegs all the way up the side. Then as your turn came to drink your fill, you knew exactly where your draught should end. This does, of course, lead one to consider whether the first drinker had to tackle the landlord about the amount of froth on his allowance which could mean he was getting short measure. Who said there's nothing new under the sun?

And what about the fights that must have broken out between drinkers – especially after a good session round the communal vessel! However, Edgar evidently meant it all for the best, because he also decreed that there should be only one system of measurement and one standard of weights in this kingdom. So at least a pint was a pint wherever you fought over it! It did sound like things might be getting out of hand though, because also at this time Edgar's Archbishop Dunstan had to ban drinking in Church!

Hundreds of years later, when the Reformation came with Henry VIII's well-known aversion to wealthy monasteries, the Church no longer had the man-power to provide the ale for a community. The job now frequently fell to the parish churchwarden, and there were often brewhouses next to churches. It seems that church fund-raising was much more exciting in those days with the ale produced being sold at 'Ale Frolics'. Sometimes events known as 'Bid Ales' or 'Help Ales' were held to collect money for a local poor man. (See how even your local pub's charity evenings have their roots in Olde Englande – although records do not say whether they had sponsored head-shaves or 'how long can you sit in a bath of cold spaghetti' evenings.) Naturally, with the Englishman's well-known moderate drinking habits, these eventually got out of hand and had to be discontinued.

A Little Diversion Concerning the Beginnings of the Art of Advertising Beer

As the centuries progressed of course, it was impossible to keep a profitable trade like the ale-house and brewing completely under control. Governments right up to the present have tried to keep it in order, whether on the grounds of finance or morality. An indication of the exasperation which inn-keepers caused the authorities is the constant fight between hosts and officials about inn-signs.

With the need to keep some kind of control over the crowded streets of the mediaeval city and the natural desire for inn-keepers to make the most of what they had, there was constant friction. In 1375 the forbears of the modern planning committee declared that no brewer should have a pole bearing his sign which projected 'more than seven feet over the highway'. And if you wanted to sell ale, you couldn't get away with not having a sign because otherwise you would forfeit your product. In the fourteenth century Richard II decreed that publicans should be legally bound to exhibit a sign; but for those of you who like to see authority in confusion, read and enjoy the new Charter for the City of London written up in the early seventeenth century. In it, the City Fathers permitted suspended inn signs but forgot to put any limit on how big they could be.

Now everyone knows that it pays to advertise. So what was more natural than each inn-keeper should try to attract custom by making his sign bigger than the one up the road. This caused massive traffic jams in the narrow wiggly streets of London! Eventually the signs in various parts of the country became just beyond a joke. (The sign at the White Hart in Norwich was said to have cost £1,000 in 1655 – in the days when you could get three pints for a penny, that represented a big investment!) Charles II tried unsuccessfully to limit the size of signs – if he had succeeded, perhaps he would have prevented a disaster of the early eighteenth century, when an oversized sign collapsed, killing two people when the house it was attached to collapsed with it!

More Attempts to Control the Brewing Industry

This attempt to regularise the building habits of the brewer was hardly a new phenomenon. In 1187, the London City Council, acutely aware that wooden buildings plus the sort of fires needed to boil water for ale, could only end in tragedy and conflagration declared that unless a brewer was prepared to invest in a stone building, he had to obtain a license for his ale-house. (As a further preventative measure they also insisted that brewsters – lady brewers – must not brew by night using sticks and straw, but only wood. This was not a sexist discriminatory act, it merely shows that only women brewed outside the monasteries.)

And so bureaucracy continued to try and tidy up the brewing industry. Magna Carta introduced standard measures for ale (but at about this time the forests were 'beyond the law' and so ale-houses in these areas could really do what they liked!) In a really sneaky piece of price fixing in 1266, the Assize of Bread and Ale tied the prices of these products to those of the raw materials. It certainly seems at this time that the brewing industry did not have a good press. In one report of the time, brewsters were mentioned along with other disreputable characters, such as nurses (!) and were condemned for wearing hoods just as though they were respectable women!

The Monarch Steps In!

Now everybody knows that beer is very important, but it's probably not as important now as it was in days gone by. Children in the fifteenth century were allowed two pints of it a day, and servants eight pints – but it was much weaker at the time. So it is not surprising that occasionally kings and queens stepped in to make sure that there was enough to go round. By the Tudors, brewing really had become an important part of the life of the Englishmen. Good Queen Bess herself declared that brewers must make and sell their beer within the financial reach of her subjects. At about the same time in London, brewers were ordered that if they 'at any time suddenly forbear and abstain from brewing whereby the King's subjects should be destitute or unprovided of drink' their equipment would be confiscated and given away to people who would brew – with the addition that these new brewers would even be given the raw materials so that they 'did not lack grains'.

How did the Hops get into Ale?

Until quite recently, it would have been quite pointless to look for fancy buildings in which to buy your ale. At this time, ale-houses were private houses with a brewing facility. Some bigger ones had their brewplant outside, but this would have been quite a sophisticated establishment. However, what was critical was the fact that beer had to be stored carefully. One of the functions of hops in beer is to act as a preservative and stabilising ingredient and there were no hops available to the mediaeval brewster, as they hadn't been imported yet. Therefore, keeping the ale in good condition was difficult. Many used a cellar to keep the liquid cool. Of course in the highlands some people used aromatic herbs to fulfil the preservative role of the hops – but in England, brewsters had to do what they could.

Now – hands up everyone who thought that beer really was the drink of Olde England, that we invented it and gave it graciously to the rest of the world? Well it wasn't quite like that – and this leads us nicely on to the next great development in ale and beer in England: the introduction of the hop. Before hops made their appearance, English ale was a heavy, sweet malt liquor, possibly not even fully fermented. It was from the low countries (now called Belgium and Holland) that this great innovation came. Until now the English had similar laws to the Reinheitsgebot so celebrated these days in Germany – in other words, nothing other than water, malt and yeast were permitted in the making of ale. Those who adulterated the product were punished – and mediaeval punishments being what they were, it was probably better to remain honest! Beer, the 'son of ale' was of course considered 'adulterated' – it contained hops, so it had to be made very clear that this was not the same drink, and that beer was different. I am now referring to this new drink as

'Beer', and by 1419 there was already mention of 'Birra' as opposed to ale – 'cervisa'. Quite who brought this new drink in is uncertain. Some people think it was soldiers who had served abroad, some people think it was merchants who had settled in London who couldn't stand English ale and wanted to import some of their own native drink. Still others reckon that it was German and Dutch merchants who knew they were on to a good thing and started brewing hopped beer in London in the fifteenth century.

But they had no easy time of it – during the fifteenth century the forerunners of the Campaign for Real Ale went to town in condemning the new brew. The city fathers of Shrewsbury went so far as to ban the 'pernicious weed' in the ale brewed in that town. As late as 1542 it was said of beer -'It is the natural drink of a Dutchman, and now of late days it is much used in England to the detriment of any English people; specially it killeth them the which be trouble with the colic, and the stone and the strangulation. For the drink is a cold drink yet it doth make a man fat, and doth inflate the belly, as it doth appear by the Dutch men's faces and bellies.'

Despite the tirade against it Beer gradually took over from ale, particularly in London and the South East. Here the German and Dutch established themselves as relatively big brewers of beer, with established brewhouses, large staffs (by fifteenth century standards – we are still not talking about breweries the size of Tetleys!). They were probably by now the same size as the larger of the small independent brewers, generally employing less than ten people. These people were known as 'Common Brewers' because they sold to the non-brewing publicans. Some however, had got the idea that a tied house was a good thing and at least one was renting a pub so as to sell his beer direct. The brewers by now had started distributing the beer themselves, so already by Tudor England it was obvious they were going to be the big business men of the future.

By this time also, the supply of hops that could be imported was inadequate, so hop fields were established in Kent (close to the beer centre of England) – the first record of their successful cultivation was in 1428.

Beer and the Law

Business may have been good for the brewer, but the law still came down hard on the publican during this period in the life of 'Merrie England'. It could be said that the authorities were pretty determined that life should not be merry at all.

The city of Canterbury declared that no beer brewed outside the walls should be sold in the city (various unscrupulous 'Scots, Irish and others' were evading local by-laws by brewing outside the walls and selling it within them). The city fathers also proclaimed that publicans should only sell their beer to those who were 'of good disposition and conversation'. Not exactly the way to build a huge trade! This may have been limiting, but you could buy three pints of ale for a penny, so there were some compensations!

It was also now that the early trading standards authorities made their presence felt. There is still an official ale-conner in the City of London who occasionally performs his duties for ceremonial purposes, but six hundred years ago it was a very important job. He would set the price of the ale, and then would answer the ale-house keeper's call to test the ale when it was ready. Once the ale had been passed fit for consumption, the ale stake was erected outside the premises and the new brew was officially on sale. Restrictions on selling the beer were very tight, and those people who did not brew on the premises were forbidden to sell ale to non-residents. With his leather trousers (used to sit on and test the ale - if the trousers stuck, the ale failed) it was his responsibility to make sure that the population of London were offered good beer. William Shakespeare's father was appointed an ale taster in Stratford upon Avon in 1556 – does this account for the number of scenes which take place in taverns in his illustrious son's plays?

There were also fines for selling beer at more than the proscribed price (who says we have progressed?) Feline fancier and Lord Mayor of London Richard Whittington slapped a £20 penalty and imprisoned miscreants who overcharged. Hooray for Richard! Legislation at this time was quite restrictive. It was also made illegal to sell beer on the streets because it was deemed that this practice would put the price up.

It was just before this time that the authorities became alarmed (yet again) at the number of ale houses in the City of London – to the extent that at one point in the sixteenth century there were only 40 in the whole city – and it was still the same square mile, but a lot drier! But you can't keep a good trade down and by a hundred years later the number of licensed premises had risen to well over 1,000. So ended another abortive attempt to control the drinking habits of the English.

As you will by now have gathered the brewing industry had already become a legislator's delight – although sometimes the laws were intended to protect rather than annoy the public. For instance street vendors were not allowed to sell ale because they would have had to buy it off the brewsters who had made it and to gain any profit they would have to put the price up, thereby 'swindling' their customers.

Of course it was still feared that the ale house would prove more attractive than the church, so it was forbidden in London to sell drink on Sundays until High Mass was finished. It was also forbidden to play games in ale-houses (because it would make people soft).

Gaming was also frowned upon in ale-houses particularly by 'poor artificers' (workmen) But the disapproval was backed by more than just a slap on the wrist – punishment for such an offence was imprisonment for three days and nights! It would be easy to call local authorities at this time spoil-sports – they even banned smoking in ale houses in Great Yarmouth (you would be taken to prison if you were caught). Which just goes to show how far sighted some of our ancestors were! There were also attempts to restrict labourers to spend only one hour of their dinner time in the inns of London because it was declared the inns did not exist to 'harbour lewd and idle people to spend and consume their money and time in lewd and drunken manner'. (In fact the punishment for drunkenness in 1606 was a five-shilling fine or six hours in the stocks – just about the time you would need to sober up!)

By the seventeenth century it had become obvious that beer was so popular that it must be a good source of income for an ever needy government. At this time, a particularly notorious character, Sir Giles Mompesson had been given the patent (or sole right) to license inns and take half of the fee.

This of course was not just a license for inns, it was also a license to print money. So Sir Guy had a very nice trade in granting permission to trade to people who had previously been banned for their unsuitability. Of course he made huge amounts of money for himself but infuriated parliament to such an extent during this time that he was eventually exiled. The relief was such when they got rid of him that the Hose of Lords declared that one day per year should be nominated a day for preaching in church to celebrate Wicked Sir Giles' expulsion.

The tax-gatherers had not always had it their own way however – an earlier attempt to levy one penny per barrel of beer produced had been blocked by the brewers' threat to go on strike, which probably would have caused a riot! This idea of taxing drink was such a good idea that the only one of Oliver Cromwell's acts that was left on the statue books when Charles II was restored to the throne was the one that referred to the taxing of beer!

I will finish my little excursion into some of the by-ways of the history of brewing at the beginning of the eighteenth century. By now the big brewers had been established and the industry had become big business. Mr Whitbread and his friends took the bulk of the production out of the hands of the small people and began to dominate the world of beer. They began to buy up pubs and to build the large empires we know today.

And the rest is history . . .

THE BIASED BREWERIES LISTING

ARCHERS ALES

London Street, Swindon, Wilts, SN1 5DG. Tel: 0793 496789

Archers Ales followed closely on the heels of Ringwood as one of the first of the new wave of small brewers who decided to set up shop in the late seventies. After fourteen years, they are still going strong, which shows a remarkable ability to weather all that economic storms can throw at small businesses, though Mark Wallingford, owner and Head Brewer modestly describes himself as 'bland'. However, since he also describes himself as a 'professional drinker' and 'rugby fanatic' perhaps the combined qualities of keen sportsman and beer expert have also contributed to his success. Mark spent some thirteen years in the RAF. When he left he needed to find a challenge equal to flying a wide variety of planes, including the huge Hercules transporters. A small brewery certainly provides that!

Mark's commercial reasons for starting a brewery are simple: 'There weren't any then except Ringwood and the Blue Anchor in Helston, and there seemed to be a terrific market opportunity.' Since Mark has also been an accountant in his time this added another set of skills needed to make a success of his business. So he set up shop in an old Railway Shed left over from the Great Western Railway and has never looked back.

The beers are:

Village Bitter	1035°
Best Bitter	1040°
Black Jack Porter	1046°
Golden Bitter	1046°
Headbanger	1065°

ARUNDEL

Unit 4D, Ford Ind. Estate, Ford, Arundel, W. Sussex. Tel: 0903 733111

When Steve Lowson and John Ryan first decided to start a brewery, it was almost for philanthropic reasons. They decided that they could not get a decent pint of independently brewed ale in their local pubs in the Arundel area and therefore they needed to make their own. They were no strangers to the world of pints since they also run one of the largest dairies in south east England, but the move from milk to milk stout was certainly new to them. However, help was on hand in the person of Fred Martin who has clocked up some fifty years of experience as head brewer of some very famous independent breweries. With Fred's help, they had soon launched several beers including Old Knucker, named after a fearsome dragon who used to eat Arundel residents.

The beers are:

Arundel Best Bitter	1040°
Arundel Stronghold	1050°
Old Knucker	1055°
Arundel Gold	1035°

ASH VINE BREWERY

White Hart, Trudoxhill, Frome, Somerset. Tel: 0373 836344

There are as many motives for setting up a small brewery as there are brewers – and the four partners at Ash Vine represent a fair selection of why people do it. Rob Viney did it because after being made redundant from his job as an industrial chemist he vowed never to work for anyone again. After a spell with Ringwood Brewery running their Frog and Frigate in Southampton learning about the trade, he and his wife Julie took over the White Hart in Trudoxhill, Somerset and found themselves on the end of Chris and Paul Clark's beer delivery service. (Paul had given up his successful business – known quaintly as 'The Mulchers' – selling bark shavings to garden centres – to start up a beer delivery service. Brother Chris had soon joined him from the world of mechanical engineering because 'it sounded like more fun').

Meanwhile, Ted Bishop (founder of the Cotleigh brewery), owner of the Bishop Brewery which made the beer which the Clarks sold to the Vineys had gone out of business, and the four between them decided to buy the equipment and set up their own brewery. And so Ash Vine was born. It soon moved in, behind the White Hart, and has gone from strength to strength. Recently, it has spread its influence to Bath in the form of a new pub – the Pig and Fiddle – and still manages to sell the vast bulk of its beer all round the country. During 1993, the brewery made a stand for the environment with a limited production of beers to make you 'drink and go green'. They had names such as Toxic Waste and Acid Rain. The intention was to raise £1000 by donating £10.00 per barrel to environmental charities for presentation in January 1994.

While you're tasting the results of this famous four's efforts you may find it illuminating to learn that Chris spends his spare time battling with the watery elements as a fanatical surfer, and one of the brewers originally came on a brewery tour from Canada and never left.

The beers are:

Trudoxhill	3.3%
Bitter	3.8%
Challenger	4.1%
Tanker*	4.7%
Hop'n'Glory	5.5%
Black Bess Porter	4.2%

*This beer is affectionately named after a former landlord of the White Hart. He dropped dead on the stairs in the pub about ten years ago after being there for many, many years.

BALLARDS BREWERY

Unit C, The Old Sawmill, Nyewood, Rogate, Petersfield, Hants, GU31 5HA.
Tel: 0730 821301

You don't normally think of an international lawyer and a 'dreadfully bad' secretary as ideal potential brewers. Yet when Mike and Carola Brown moved to the country Mike also decided that he no longer wanted to commute, so they had to look around for a business which they could run from their new home. Luckily a life long interest in beer and an old cowshed prompted the idea to run a brewery. Mike was the leading force and Carola helped with administration and telephone selling. It prospered and they moved the business to the village pub which Carola ran as her contribution to the operation.

As they overcame teething troubles and the business began to run smoothly, Mike began to yearn for his old life as a legal eagle and the brewery was threatened with closure. However, the prospect of returning to the uneventful life of a housewife did not appeal to Carola, and she took the business on as her own (it had after all been given her maiden name, since they had decided that Brown was a little too ordinary). After that, it moved from the pub to a small industrial estate, and has since become remarkably well-known (particularly for the Christmas pub walks and the annual escalation in strength of the Christmas beer). Carola's claim to real fame was the day when she opened the *Daily Mail* and discovered in a book

review that she had been included in a book of ecological heros. Since the list also included Prince Charles, she felt that at least she was keeping good company, although it has never been explained to her what she had actually done, apart from running her brewery!

The beers are:

Midhurst Mild	1035°	
Trotton Bitter	1036°	
Best Bitter	1042°	
Wassail	1060°	
Old Episcopal	1092°	(bottled, but nearly all gone)

THE BEER ENGINE

Newton St. Cyres, Exeter, S. Devon, EX5 5AX. Tel: 0392 851282

Peter Hawksley woke up one morning, ten years ago, and decided he could not go on as he was. After twenty years of teaching English, Sociology and Communications to college students, he thought "I think I'll run a brewery!" He actually wanted a brewpub. So, when a run-down pub called the Olde Barne Owle came on the market in Newton St Cyres near Exeter, he set about installing a brewery and creating a whole new pub. It was perfect. So perfect, in fact, that in 1992 he celebrated brewing his millionth pint of beer. Although he unassumingly claims that his beers win only modest local prizes, they have built up a solid reputation all round the country. Evidence of this was a lunchtime party held by 16 senior railway officials who had gathered in the Beer Engine to celebrate their retirement. They had come from all over the south of England and eventually enjoyed themselves so much that they missed their five o'clock train home!

The brewery's reputation is not only national, for Peter revealed that he was invited to France with 30 kilderkins to take part in the annual Caen Fair. Reaction to his beer was favourable, but he commented darkly on the dubious French refrigeration equipment. 'I'll take my own next time'. The Beer

Engine's other claim to fame is their knack of inventing names for their beers which are then borrowed by other people. Their Piston Bitter and Rail Ale have both spawned namesakes. So has their Sleeper, although no-one else has had the suffix Heavy attached to it. Perhaps the Scottish customer who made the name-change will not drink it anywhere else. (The names owe their railway flavour to the brewpub's proximity to the train line).

The beers are:

Rail Ale	1037°
Piston Bitter	1044°
Sleeper Heavy	1055°
Whistlemas	1068°

BLACKAWTON BREWERY

Washbourne, Totnes, S. Devon, TQ9 7UF. Tel: 0803 732339

Barry Quiggan did not start his own brewery. Blackawton was originally the brainchild of an eccentric who had opted for the 'good life' in Devon. This gentleman however did not devote as much time to the brewery as he might have done, and therefore his beer gained a reputation for inconsistency. But sometimes it was truly magnificent. At this time Barry Quiggan used to come down to the family retreat in Devon and he would look forward to a pint. And then the brewery came up for sale. Barry, who was commuting from London to Devon and getting heartily sick of it, was looking for an opportunity to start a business with a bit of rural peace built in.

After the initial shock at the thought of buying a brewery, Barry took the business on and he now claims that he has the most beautiful brewery garden in England (the brewery is in a barn next to the house). The time for a brewery visit is apparently May, when the azaleas are out. The property borders on Dartmoor (which occasionally tries to encroach in the form of some sheep and a particular nosy local bullock) and the Quiggan family now have all the rural surroundings they could want. But

Barry still has an eye on the outside world, with great plans for the brewery. 'We are still very small, averaging around 20 barrels per week, but eventually I would like to experiment with some very different beers, such as Belgian-type fruit beer. Devon is very food conscious,' he continues, 'and if we can bottle something a little out of the ordinary, I think it will go down very well here.'

The beers are:

Blackawton Bitter	1037°
Devon Gold	1040°
44 Special	1044°
Headstrong	1051°

BLEWITT'S

Ship and Plough, Kingsbridge, S. Devon. Tel: 0548 852485

No-one can say that Steve Blewitt has not had long enough to learn how to brew beer. He showed his early entrepreneurial skills at the age of 10 brewing up from brew-kits and selling his product to his father for pocket money. This has all come in handy in the six years that he has been running the Ship and Plough in South Devon, even his 'brewhouse' was originally positioned behind the bar in the pub.

During this period of experimentation, he was trying to recapture the skills he had developed as a ten-year old. Naturally, this caused a great deal of interest in the pub, as people were attracted by the smell of brewing beer and came in to see what was going on. It caused less interest from Her Majesty's Customs and Excise however, who, when informed by Steve that he was starting to brew commercially, but was only producing some five gallons at a time, told him to come back when he 'had got a bit bigger'. Well, he has. He has a newly-installed five-barrel brew plant, with a 90 gallon copper he designed himself (years as a plant maintenance engineer in the dairy industry has helped here). And what next? At the moment he is still content with his new plant, but someone who started as a brewer at the age of 10 can't possibly stop there!

The beers are:

Blewitt's Best Bitter	1040°	
Blewitt's Head Off	1050°	
King's	1038°	(Occasional)

BLUE ANCHOR

50 Coinagehall Street, Helston, Cornwall, TR13 8EL Tel: 0326 562821

At some time in the fourteenth century the monks in Helston, Cornwall felt the need to brew their beer, which they did quite happily until Henry VIII decided that he required their premises as necessary to his master plan to reform the Church in England. Three hundred years later, part of the former monastery became the Blue Anchor Inn and it was discovered that if they wanted beer in it the new owners had better brew it themselves. The tradition of brewing at the pub has since then been uninterrupted. The present owners, the Richards family, has held the property for 150 years. In 1993, the present tenants, Simon Stone and Kim Corbett, have taken over from 73-year old Sid Cannon who had been there for fifteen years. The Blue Anchor's fame over the years has grown to the extent that they now need to brew up to 30 barrels per week in the summer – all for sale in the tiny pub and locally known as 'Spingo'. The pub is also well known for the strength of its beer – there is a famous story of the American who was acquitted for drinking and driving locally because the Magistrate realised that the man had not known the potency of Sid's beer. Sid himself had to make an appearance in court to explain the different levels of strength of different beers.

The beers are:

Medium Bitter	1050°
Best Bitter	1053°
Special Bitter	1066°
Extra Special	1076°

BORDER BREWERY

The Old Kiln, Brewery Lane, Berwick upon Tweed, TD15 2AH. Tel: 0289 303303

All beer drinkers should be very grateful that the owners of the Border Brewery Co in Berwick changed their mind about their first products. When Tony Reeman-Clark and Alan Crawford originally decided in the local pub that they were going to set up in business they were going to sell the water from their well in bottles. Later, they decided that the seventeenth century building which houses the brewery should go back to its original and intended use. (This may have had the further benefit of appeasing the ghost who haunts the premises, because he or she hasn't been seen since the brewery opened).

The work is very evenly divided, with the two women in the company, Mandy Reeman-Clark and Carol Crawford doing all the brewing, while their husbands do the marketing, which involves visiting all the pubs. They are relatively self-sufficient with Anthony using his expertise as a computer consultant to produce all the pump-clip designs and letterheads on their own equipment. They also still keep up their outside occupations while running the brewery.

The brewery itself dates from the seventeenth century and, if they should decide they need inspiration, they can just go round the corner to consult the gravestone of a former head brewer who died in 1801. Fortunately for them, Hadrian's Brewery up the road, has also been a great help while being considerably easier to contact. Since none of them had ever brewed before, it required enormous effort to bring their level of knowledge up to the required standard but all seems to be going well, with their beer selling in Newcastle and Glasgow. In 1993, they took over a local pub, the Angel Inn, which was one of the original brewery's tied houses. Is history repeating itself?

The beers are:

Old Kiln Bitter	1036°
Old Kiln Ale	1038°

BRANSCOMBE VALE BREWERY

Great Seaside Farm, Branscombe, Devon, EX12 3DP. Tel: 0297 80511

Graham Luxton had been thinking of starting a brewery for over eight years before Branscombe Brewery was born. Perhaps it was lucky that he waited until late 1992 to set it up, because he and his partner Paul Dimond now have an idyllic brewhouse in an idyllic setting only yards from a Devon beach. They occupy two old stone barns with seagulls and a thatched reed company for neighbours and the National Trust for landlords. 'At first they were a bit wary of our using these barns for a business', commented Graham, 'but once they were satisfied that we were responsible people, they could not have been more helpful.'

The decision to start the brewery was forced on Graham and Paul when the dairy firm they worked for folded – but the stainless steel pipework that they managed to rescue from the company has stood them in good stead, although it is more likely to be used for milk stout than the sort that comes from cows! Paul's previous experience with one of the large cider manufacturers also came in useful. Another great help to the new business is Graham's wife's family pub which she runs in Branscombe village nearby. The Fountain Head is not owned by the brewery but Catharine Luxton can always be relied on to take Graham's beer. I suppose this means that he takes his work home with him, but the pub's customers certainly seem to appreciate it! Since starting the brewery Graham has become an even stronger supporter of beer produced by

his fellow small brewers. 'If I can't get beer from a brewery like mine', he declares, 'then I won't drink beer at all!'

The beers are:

Brannoc	1040°
Olde Stoker	1055°

BREWERY-ON-SEA

24 Winston Business Centre, Chartwell Road, Lancing, W. Sussex, BN15 8TU
Tel: 0903 851482

Rob Jones and John Sale are not new to the brewing industry, despite their brewery only being a few months old. Rob was responsible for the Champion Beer of Britain, Dark Star when he was at the Pitfield Street Brewery and John Sales is the author of 'Beer on Bikes' (which unfortunately missed publication when the publisher went bankrupt). However, they now run the Brewery-on-Sea in Lancing, West Sussex. They boast an early background in home brewing but Rob began his career as a Civil Servant, a postman and 'various other things which I didn't enjoy'. John had two years as a trainee Chartered Accountant before he realised that it really wasn't what he wanted to do.

John's accountancy training made him cautious about launching into brewing without some trial runs and this was how he came across Rob. Rob had moved the Pitfield Brewery up to Stourbridge and John approached him for some contract brewing. When the Pitfield Brewery finally disappeared, the two decided to combine forces to run a brewery down on the South Coast. John had always wanted this as his location, and Rob already had a flat in Brighton – they were obviously destined to get together! (Although it took two years to eventually set it all up!) Since then they have started up the 80 barrel capacity plant and have enjoyed success right from the beginning. Their

beers are aptly named to have a sailing (or local) connection. The only difficulty so far has been that the two brewers are run off their feet!

The beers are:

Spinnaker Mild	3.5%
Spinnaker Bitter	3.5%
Spinnaker Classic	4.0%
Special Crew	5.5%
Black Rock	5.5%
Riptide	6.5%

BRIDGWATER BREWING COMPANY

Unit 1, Lovedere Farm, Goathurst, Bridgwater, Somerset. TA5 2DD.
Tel: 0278 663996

When Jeff Lucas lost his job as a watch-maker in February 1992 there seemed only one option for him to take as a new career. After twenty years as an avid home brewer he had always wanted to try his hand at the 'real thing' so he decided to set up a brewery. Nothing very unusual in that you say – but Jeff is partially disabled because of a bout of polio as a child.

He is not wheelchair bound, by any means but brewing is a particularly physical occupation, so does he find this a problem? 'It is hard', he says, 'but if you don't take on things which you really can't do, it's amazing what you can achieve. For instance, I have been banned from loading the barrels onto the delivery truck, since I nearly dropped one on my colleague's toe, but apart from that I seem to manage quite well. The brewery is on two levels, and it is tiring, but we all get tired don't we?' Jeff would like to think that his experiences will encourage other disabled people to have a go at something that is a challenge. 'It's important not to just lie down and give up' he says. The five-barrel brewery started operations in April 1993, and in the first few months appreciative things were being said about their Amber and Sunbeam Ales. 'It's very satisfying' commented Jeff. When he's not lugging nine gallon casks around the brewery, Jeff relaxes as a sub-aqua diver at a local club.

The beers are:

Carnival	1035°	(Available annually in October and November)
Amber	1040°	
Coppernob	1045°	
Sunbeam	1052°	

BUNCE'S BREWERY

The Old Mill, Mill Lane, Netheravon, Wilts, SP4 9QB. Tel:0980 70631

Forget Hamlet (the Danish prince who liked to say "maybe") and a certain Danish lager company who frequently say "probably". Stig Andersen was one Dane who was absolutely sure that a small independent brewery in a tiny village in Wiltshire was the place for him. He first saw it a year ago, lured by an advertisement in a small British trade magazine. All it said was "Brewery for sale – fed up with brewing" and Stig followed the path of his Viking ancestors and was on the next boat over. One look at the charming building and one taste of the beers and he decided that he would move himself and his young family to the English countryside and start producing traditional English beers. This was going to be a welcome change from his life in Denmark as the managing director and master brewer of a small subsidiary of a very large brewery, where he produced what he calls "tastless, cheap lager". After only a few months he is settled, delighted with the warm welcome he received from his fellow villagers and looking forward to maintaining Bunce's excellent standards (and their beers). He speaks for himself:

"The reason why we decided to take up the challenge to buy a small brewery in Britain is because the British have a beer-culture with room for small breweries and good ale. We have been very lucky to find Bunce's Brewery and we are very much looking to supplying the British beer drinkers with Stig's good ale brewed after Tony Bunce's excellent prescriptions." Who can tell – maybe in the future Stig will be able to add his special Danish touch to the British ale. "But it is not only because of the beer we moved to Britain," says Stig. "We are also very fond of the British humour and mentality which we find is quite similar to the Danish. We promise the British people that we are not mean and savage Vikings but decent people who are looking forward to living and acting in good, old beautiful Britain."

The Danes may have said "No" to Maastricht, but here's one who said a very definite "Yes" to Netheravon!

The beers are:

Bench Mark	1035°
Pig Swill	1040°
Best Bitter	1042°
Old Smokey	1050°

(The Wheat Beer is on the price list, but unless there is an increase in demand in it, that's where it will stay. Tony Bunce, the previous owner, kept the name simply because he was fond of the beer – although very few pubs seemed to order it!)

BURTON BRIDGE BREWERY

Bridge Street, Burton on Trent, DE14 1SY. Tel: 0283 510573

Jeff Mott's career must be close to every school boy's dream. From his early days as an apprentice to Rolls Royce, through his career as a test engineer on military aircraft, and a short spell with an explosives company he has also fulfilled a lot of grown up boys' dreams by running his own brewery (with partner Bruce Wilkinson) for the past twelve years. (In between he also ran a pig farm for three years, but that's another story!) The brewery story started many years ago when Bruce and Jeff worked together at Romford Brewery in London and became convinced that small breweries were a viable prospect. They also decided that neither of them could afford to set one up individually so it was obvious they should go into partnership.

The location of the brewery was easy – Burton-on-Trent is the centre of the British brewing industry, so where better? The actual building was discovered during a business trip to the town. Jeff excused himself from lunch and leapt over the wall of a boarded-up pub to find the ideal premises. There was little competition for the place since most people had no idea what they were going to do with "all the extra buildings". But Jeff and Bruce knew exactly what they were going to do with them! Once they had got the brewery up and running, they got fed up with people asking them when they were going to open the pub, so for the princely sum of £1000 they quickly patched up the bar and opened to the public, and it was an instant hit. Despite their big brewery colleagues warning them that they would not last six months on their own, they are increasingly successful. They are now too busy to run the pub themselves so it is a very successful tenancy. (It is said that the pews which serve as seating come out of the chapel where Harold Wilson's parents were married.)

Of course, after twelve years the stories that Jeff recalls are many, but he fondly remembers being locked up in a police cell for couple of hours on Christmas Eve to cool his heels after a particularly zealous bout of debt collecting. He was not charged, but he says that they now have very few bad debts! As if to belie this rather fierce story, the brewery has one golden rule, they start every day "with a jolly good laugh, and if possible finish with one as well!"

The beers are:

XL Bitter	1040°	named after Burton's Roman heritage (the pub is next to an archeological site inscribed with the numerals XL).
Bridge Bitter	1042°	
Burton Porter	1045°	
Burton Festival	1055°	
Summer:		
Summer Ale	1038°	
Top Dog Ale	1050°	(named after the Stafford-shireBull Terrier)
Winter:		
Old Expensive	1065°	
Christmas:		
Hearty Ale	1050°	

BUSHEY'S BREWERY

Mount Murray, Braddan, Isle of Man. Tel: 0624 661244

When Martin Brunschweiler popped up to see his sister eight years ago, he only meant to stay for the weekend. Now four pubs and a brewery later he finds it hard to remember that he only came up to the Isle of Man originally to help his sister out with a few sandwiches when she opened up her new pub. Having just returned from Australia he had intended to go back to London to pursue his own career as a chef. One thing, however, led to another, and eventually he found that he could not get cask beer supplied to the pub by the local brewery, and it was too expensive to ship it from the mainland. The only option of course was for Martin to brew his own. Conveniently, the Brighton Brewery sold up its equipment just at the right time although it did mean that there had to be some emergency building work in the cellar to fit the plant in. Since those days Martin has acquired three more pubs and he has benefited yet again from other people being 'uncooperative'.

The council turned the road in front of Bushey's into a pedestrian piazza, which Martin at first thought would kill his trade, so he opposed it strongly. Luckily he failed and he is now delighted with the new open space, which has become a popular beer garden, particularly during TT Week when bikers use his pub as a convenient rendezvous. Motorcyclists have also led to another innovation for Martin and Bushey's brewery, since they now intend to bottle their Piston Bitter for sale to the biking community (but only when they are on two legs rather than two wheels). His other pubs on the Isle of Man are the Rover's Return (yes, really), and the Duck's Nest, Castleton. But what about Martin's ambitions as a chef – does he still hanker after creating culinary masterpieces? 'Well, actually no,' admitted Martin. 'We do food in the pubs, but quite honestly, I don't like going into the kitchen if I can help it – I'd much rather be in the brewery!'

The beers are:

Dark Mild	1035°
Best Bitter	1038°
Piston Brew	1045°
Old Bushy Tail	1045°
Lovely Jubbely	1060°

BUTCOMBE BREWERY

Butcombe, Bristol, BS18 6XQ. Tel: 027547 2240

You would probably have to know it was there to find Butcombe Brewery, hidden as it is among the leafy lanes of the rural outskirts of Bristol. Housed in an eighteenth century farmhouse, it is certainly a different view of the brewing industry from the one which was familiar to Simon Whitmore before he became a 'small independent brewer'. Managing Director of Courage Western, Marketing Director of Guinness Malaysia and General Manager for Courage in Australia had been some of Simon's titles.

When starting the brewery in 1978 his headcount went down to three – himself, his wife Maureen, and a neighbour's son. Butcombe's success is well-known among cask-conditioned ale enthusiasts. They are now one of the largest small independent brewers, producing over 200 barrels per week. But their beginnings were as tough as everybody else's, with initial battles with planning committees (until they convinced them that brewing was a rural craft and completely appropriate for farm outbuildings) and the purchase of second-hand equipment that bigger brewers no longer wanted.

There were of course also some early disasters, but publicans seemed to like the beer (even though Simon didn't) and kept clamouring for more, to the extent that Butcombe's single beer is just the same as it was fifteen years ago. The plant has grown steadily, with the third and final expansion from 45 to 80 barrel capacity coinciding with Simon's sixtieth birthday. Incidentally, this is the first time they have ever bought brand-new equipment. The company has now grown to a payroll of eight but the brewing staff still rotate their duties, every evening playing spoof to decide who is going to do what on the following day. The Whitmores were told when they first started the brewery that it would be like getting on an escalator, once on it was impossible to get off – but I don't think they really ever wanted to!

The beer is:

Butcombe Bitter 1039°

BUTTERKNOWLE BREWERY

Old School House, Lynesack, Bishop Auckland, Co. Durham, DM13 5QF.
Tel: 0388 710109

Noel Coward warned parents not to put their children on the stage. Little did Mrs Constable know that her son John's theatrical experience would eventually lead him into the equally interesting world of small brewing. When John Constable met his wife Susan he was involved in theatrical management, but the inherent insecurity of show-business and Susan's impending redundancy as a local government officer forced them to look elsewhere to earn a living.

In the mid-eighties they bought a pub in North Shields called the Chainlocker which rose re-born from a state of dilapidation to become one of the best known watering holes in the North East. The experience gave the Constables the idea of venturing into the rapidly expanding world of real ale, thinking it would give them a less frantic lifestyle. 'Fat Chance!', says John. He was in fact a complete novice when he started the brewery. 'I had never seen a brewery working until the first time we brewed here at Butterknowle.' However, they found themselves the Old School House at Lynesack, which was in splendid condition, although the school buildings which were destined to become the brewery itself were in a sorry state, having lain untouched for some thirty years. Since those days the brewery has doubled in size to a

20 barrel plant with outlets spread right across the country, and with a delivery service that stretches as far down south as Cambridgeshire and Bristol. To make sure that the brewery is tied in securely with local history the Constables also made use of the old Miner's Banners from the long defunct Woodland and Butterknowle collieries as the inspiration for their pump clips and beer mats.

The beers are:

Bitter	1036°
Festival Stout	1038°
Conciliation Ale	1042°
Black Diamond	1050°
High Force	1060°
Old Ebenezer	1080°

CHILTERN

Nash Lee Road, Terrick, Aylesbury, Bucks, HP17 0TQ. Tel: 0296 613647

Most breweries can claim a first prize for their bitter or their porter at a beer festival at some time – but very few get one for their cheese at a County Show. Chiltern Brewery, however, since they started some ten years ago have done more than just brew beer – they have expanded into selling mustards, pickled onions and even cakes (and the cheeses) all based on their three bitters and their barley wine. Richard and Lesley Jenkinson first cleared out the barns on their small farm in rural Buckinghamshire with the express idea of being able to run a business from home so that Richard would not have to commute to the City each day to work in the Financial Markets. As enthusiastic home brewers they, of course, intended to set up a brewery primarily. The planning restrictions on their property, however, meant that at first they also had to have an agricultural side to the business. This was why they had to breed rabbits at first. Of course, rabbits being what they are they threatened to take over the whole of the brewery, and it was decided they simply had to go. The Jenkinsons do not seem to have missed the rabbits and they have a thriving 15 barrel capacity brewery and a well-stocked brewery shop. They have also devised a programme of well-organised brewery visits which finish with a slap up lunch comprising the brewery's own products. The latest acquisition in 1992 put them into competition with some much bigger breweries – they have the use of a pair of Percheron horses and now have a brewery dray to take their name to local summer events and give rides at brewery open days.

The beers are:

Chiltern Ale	1038°
Beechwood Bitter	1043°
Three Hundreds Old Ale	1050°
Bodgers Barley Wine	1080°

COACH HOUSE BREWERY COMPANY LTD

Wharf Street, Warrington, Cheshire, WA1 2DQ. Tel: 0925 232800

The original intention was that Neil Chantrell, who had just been made redundant from Greenall Whitley, and his wife should run a brewery on their own. It was also originally intended that they run it in the coach house behind their home. Unfortunately (or fortunately) when three of Neil's colleagues were also made redundant, they came round and asked him about his new venture. And so the Coach House Brewery expanded and grew before it had even started. That was two years ago, and now the 140 barrel per week plant is successfully producing beer which is sold all round the country (including to one of the North West's major brewing concerns).

The beer is available in around some 400 outlets (including at Heathrow Airport, in case you need a last taste of British Bitter before you leave these shores) and remarkably enough the Coach House Brewery manages to supply 200 of them direct with its own dray. 'It does mean that the lorry has to leave at 3.30 a.m. some mornings', explained Neil, 'and that all the five working directors have to be able to deliver beer, as well as do their own specific jobs – but that's what being part of a small brewery is all about'. Neil was head brewer at Greenall Whitley for 26 years, so it was interesting to hear that what he appreciated mostly was the freedom now to buy whatever malting barley and hops he thought were best, and hang the expense. ' It maybe adds 50p to the cost of a barrel of beer, which is not much to a small producer – of course if I had done that when I worked for a large company the bill would have run into the millions, so it's a real benefit for our customers.' He also enjoys the freedom to brew all sorts of special beers for special occasions. 'In 1992 we did about ten different beers with four or five "occasion" brews. We did Valentine's Night beers, Burns Night Beers and the publicans loved them. They take them without knowing what they're going to taste like, but they keep coming back for more, so they are obviously happy!' Their confidence is obviously well-placed. At the 1993 Great British Beer Festival, their Blunderbus won the Porters and Stouts class.

The beers produced are:

Coachman's Best Bitter	1037°
Ostler's SPA	1038°
Squires Gold	1042°
Innkeeper's Special Reserve	1045°
Blunderbus Old Porter	1055°

CONCERTINA BAND CLUB BREWERY

13 Hampden Road, Mexborough, S. Yorks. Tel: 0709 580841

Even the name behind this brewery is interesting and authentic, and the story behind it is curious and fascinating. Concertina bands, apparently, although now not so celebrated as the splendid brass bands, provided a more modest outlet for working men's musical talents. They were particularly popular in the North of England in the last century, and in Mexborough, South Yorkshire, Andy Pickering now runs the local Concertina Band Club with his mother and his brother-in-law, Alan Boyd. The Club was bought specifically because of its capacious cellars which could accommodate a small brewery. However, it took six years to start the brewery and it was only after Andy's late father had spent the previous year urging them on, that production started. Andy recalls, with sadness tinged with pride, that they had just achieved their first successful test brew just before his father had his fatal heart attack. 'At least he knew we had achieved our ambition' he says. Mr Pickering Senior would be even more pleased if he knew how popular the resulting beer has proved. Despite brewing three times per week they can still only just keep up with demand from club-members, although they have recently installed a larger 5-barrel brew plant in the cellar.

On the musical front, Andy regrets that the last surviving member of the Band plays a different sort of concertina to him, and although he also admits that his talent as a brewer is more than as a musician, he still enjoys pushing out a tune or two during quiet moments (which are very rare!). The quality of the beer however has without doubt proved beneficial to at least this last band member. In 1993, at the age of 77 he got married. No doubt they chose to toast his health in Club Bitter in preference to Champagne!

The beers are:

Concertina Best Bitter	1038°
Concertina Festival Ale	1042°
Concertina Bandsman Strong Ale	1040°

COTLEIGH BREWERY

Ford Road, Wiveliscombe, Somerset, TA4 2RE. Tel: 0984 24086

Cotleigh Brewery may be the only brewery in the country which receives calls asking about the nesting habits of Tawny Owls. This is because Cotleigh's owners, Jennifer and John Aries, over the last three years have worked very closely with The Hawk and Owl Trust which works to protect Britain's birds of prey and the countryside in which they live. In fact, John can thank his very own 'Tawny' for bringing him and Jennifer together. When she worked in the local pub, as a newly arrived Australian, he asked her for a pint of Cotleigh. She had no idea what he was talking about, so offered him a pint of Tawny, saying 'It's very popular with the locals'. She says herself, 'Would he have found me so attractive if I had offered him a pint of Carling Black Label?'

The brewery itself was founded in a stable block on Cotleigh Farm 1979 near Tiverton, and moved sometime later to purpose built premises in Wiveliscombe in Somerset. John Aries took over some 10 years ago and now the brewery is a thriving business employing five people and producing 100 barrels per week. They supply around 120 pubs in Somerset and Devon and their beers are available across the country through selected wholesalers. These days, the Aries are proud to be associated with the Hawk and Owl Trust, sponsoring collecting boxes in local pubs and helping raise much needed cash for the cause. All their beer mats carry details of the trust, and all the beers are named after birds of prey. So if you have a question for Cotleigh they are equally happy if it is about birds as beer! (Please note that Cotleigh shares the tiny hometown of Wiveliscombe with their near neighbours, Exmoor Ales.)

Their beers are:

Harrier SPA	1036°
Nutcracker Mild	1036°
Tawny Bitter	1040°
Aldercote Ale	1042°
Barn Owl Bitter	1048°
Old Buzzard	1048°
Rebellion	1050°
Red Nose Reinbeer	1060°

COTTAGE BREWERY

Little Orchard, West Lydford, Somerset, TA11 7DQ. Tel: 096324 383

When you talk about high-flyers in the brewing industry, Chris Norman of the Cottage Brewing Company must qualify, because he is an airline pilot. Formerly Chief Pilot with Britannia Airways, he opted for relocation to Somerset so that he could eventually open his own brewery in what he calls 'this haven of real ale'. He had not expected to be able to start up properly so soon since he is still quite a few years off retirement, but an 'early severance' scheme has enabled him to make his dream reality immediately. One thing he has noticed is that brewing is not a soft option as a retirement plan – it really is hard work!

Chris is not a newcomer to brewing, having been introduced to beer making at an early age by his father. He spent the last twenty to thirty years as a full-mash home brewer but this is his first venture into ale-making on a large scale. His very first brew was snapped up immediately by local publicans and the four barrel brew plant will soon be in operation twice per week. The Cottage Brewery is so named partly to convey the idea of a 'cottage industry' and partly because the garage it is housed in looks like a cottage. It is next to the Normans' house, so at least won't have to travel round the world to get to work like he does now!

The beers are:

S&D*	4.4%	
Norman's Conquest	1066°	(for Christmas)

*After the Somerset and Dorset Railway, a former local line much loved by natives of those two counties.

CROUCH VALE BREWERY LTD

12 Redhills Road, South Woodham, Chelmsford, Essex, CM3 5UP.
Tel: 0245 322744

Colin Bocking, at Crouch Vale, reckons he started his brewing career on the other side of the bar. 'My drinker's dream of brewing my own beer simply went too far'. So thirteen years ago he and his partner (who no longer takes an active part in the business) set up in an industrial unit near Chelmsford and they have grown steadily ever since, until now they have a capacity of some ninety barrels per week. The brewery has also since acquired their own pub, The Cap and Feathers in Tillingham, Essex – which as Colin will proudly you tell is a former CAMRA National Pub of the Year. The other thing about the brewery that has grown over the years is the list of beers. They now have seven or eight different beers to choose from which, as Colin points out, is an administrative nightmare, but much more fun than just having one or two. 'The problem is that we brew beers which people like and they keep coming back to buy more of them, so we can't let them down!' Colin must be the envy of many brewers because despite running such a busy business it does not preclude him from pursuing his interests in cricket, music, computers and wine.

The beers are:

Best Mild	1036°
Best Bitter	1039°
Millenium Ale	1041°
SAS (Strong Anglian Special)	1048°
Essex Porter	1050°
Santa's Revenge	1055°
Willy Warmer	1060°

DALESIDE BREWERY

Camwal Road, Starbeck, Harrogate, N. Yorks. HG1 4PT. Tel: 0423 880041

Bill Witty originally came up with the idea of a brewery because he knew an out-of-work microbiologist. When a brewery came up for sale locally it seemed an ideal opportunity for the microbiologist to start a new business with Bill as a partner. The microbiologist 'shook and shivered' at the state of the premises, which since Bill had a building firm really did not present much of a problem at the time. Unfortunately, by the time they had done the work, the microbiologist had finally cried off and Bill was left with a brewery but no brewer. Eventually, Bill found himself a brewer but by this time the property boom bubble had burst and taken its toll, leaving Bill with a brewery which had to pay for itself.

To cut short a long and painful story, after enormous problems Bill moved premises and his new brewer also made an unexpected disappearance. Bill has now been joined by Craig, one of his two sons (ironically, the son who is a fully qualified brewer is now working in San Francisco). Craig is currently learning the business and the brewery is growing steadily. Over the years not only have the premises changed for the brewery but also some names of the beers. Piston Bitter and Old Lubrication are now known as Daleside and Dalesman Old Ale but Monkey Wrench still retains its old name. (This beer was originally brewed for a beer festival, and was known as Monkey Hanger after an unfortunate incident in the 13th Century when a monkey was mistaken for a French spy and duly executed).

The beers are:

Daleside	1038°
Dalesman Old Ale	1042°
Monkey Wrench	1056°

DENT BREWERY

Hollins, Cowgill, Dent, Cumbria, LA10 5TQ. Tel: 05396 25326

Martin Stafford thinks it is significant that his first beer went on sale on 1st April 1990. He eventually came to brewing having made the brave decision that he was completely unemployable by anybody. A former Managing Director of a large chain of petrol stations he has an unenviable track record of being made redundant and being sacked in the same year. All that was left, he concluded was to work for himself. Since he was fond of beer and the countryside, the next obvious step was to buy a pub in a remote part of Cumbria and enjoy his independence. As his family outgrew the accommodation in the pub they moved to an old farmhouse nearby which happened to have two old barns as outhouses. The buildings needed refurbishing so he looked around for something useful to do with them. Although his first thought was to make chocolate, the businessman in him suggested that there may be a limited market in such remote Fell country – but as he had his own pub, why not produce his own beer? It was his ambition to make something he liked and which was fun, so brewing fulfilled all the criteria. A consultation with local brewery expert David Smith eventually came to fruition and Dent Bitter was born.

The brewery has since doubled capacity and they have added Ramsbottom and Awd Tup to their range. Martin is, however, determined to stay with just three beers to ensure that they are always available. 'Ramsbottom is particularly popular, maybe because the name conjures up the whole spirit of the countryside hereabouts – there are certainly a lot of sheep! We use local spring water which comes off the Fells, and the view is magnificent.' Brother Nick also brews not too far away (see Hambleton Brewery).

The beers are:

Dent Bitter	1036°
Ramsbottom Strong Ale	1044°
Awd Tup	1055°

EARL SOHAM BREWERY

1 Cobbolds Row, Earl Soham, Woodbridge, Suffolk, IP13 7RL.
Tel: 0728 685894

Becoming a brewer had been John Bjornsen's dream since he left school. But unfortunately, his lack of formal qualifications stopped the large brewers benefiting from his natural talents, and they rejected his early applications. But several years later, after taking himself through university as a mature student, the now well-qualified chemist decided that he was going to become a brewer without their help. Originally he and his wife and his brother (a vet by profession) took on the Victoria pub in the village of Earl Soham, Suffolk in 1985 as a paying hobby. There were some suitable out-buildings behind the pub and very soon John was cobbling together his own brew plant to provide the pub with its own beer. They also had a pub in Cambridge which John's brother built himself, cellar upwards. It soon became obvious that there was not enough profit to support them all in the enterprise, so John's brother has gone back to veterinary work, remaining as a partner and keeping a keen interest in the business. The Earl Soham produces between 5 and 15 barrels per week depending on demand, although John only sells outside the pub strictly by request than by design. If you want some of his beer for a party, you'll have to go and ask him to brew it for you! This is deliberate; John got rid of his delivery van when they gave up the second pub, and does not regret the loss. As well as the list of beers given below, Jolabrugg is produced every winter as a Christmas beer, but it is no use asking John what its strength will be or how it will taste. 'Each brew depends on how I feel', he says. 'It's very popular – but I don't like it myself!' The Victoria itself is designed for people who hate music and games machines – John won't have these noisy modern distractions on the premises!

The beers are:

Gannet Mild	1032.5°
Victoria Bitter	1036.5°
Albert	1044.5°
Jolabrugg	1060°

EVESHAM

The Green Dragon, Oat Street, Evesham, Worcester, R11 4J. Tel: 0386 446337

A publican by profession, Steven Murphy knew there was something missing in Evesham and decided to fill the gap himself. He had seen micro-breweries successfully operating elsewhere, and decided to give the town what it had lacked since the closing of the old Rowlands Brewery some forty-five years ago. Since then, in 1993, when he opened his five-barrel plant behind his pub, The Green Dragon, he has been proved right. Lager drinkers are being converted to the taste of real ale; he sells out as soon as the beer is ready.

The brewery is an integral part of the attraction of the pub, built to be seen, and housed in a former bottle store. The venture is also adding to the tourist attractions of the town, which is famous for the site of the battle where Simon de Montfort, founder of the English Parliamentary system, died in 1265. Steve has opened a function room above the pub, which boasts a spectacular mural of the battle and together with the Simon de Montfort Society is producing leaflets to help attract more visitors to the town. At the moment the beer, Asum Ale, is only available in the Green Dragon and in Steve's other pub, The Dugout also in Evesham, but there are plans to sell it through carefully selected rural pubs in the future. (There is no doubt that the beer is popular, it is beginning to attract visitors from Manchester and Essex who are expressly visiting the town to try the beer!) Why, you may ask, is it called Asum Ale? Because in local dialect that is what they call Evesham.

The beers are:

Asum Ale	1038°
Asum's Gold	1050°

EXE VALLEY BREWERY

Silverton, Nr Exeter, Devonshire, EX5 4HF. Tel: 0392 860406

Exe Valley and sheep seem to cross paths remarkably often. It could be said that they brought the brewery into being. The first partner in the present team, Richard Barron, was a landlord at the Three Tuns, in Silverton, Devon, but he fancied himself as a sheep farmer and bought a farm in the district. Unfortunately, an accident with a JCB limited his capacity to run up and down hills after the sheep so he decided to turn his talents to beer again and become a brewer. He converted a cowshed into the brewhouse and the business that was later to become the Exe Valley Brewery was born in 1984. Meanwhile, the other partner, Guy Shepherd (see – they can't get away from sheep) had turned away from a life of accountancy after graduating from Exeter University and become a beer wholesaler, a business which he sold in 1991. Meanwhile, Richard Barron's Brewery had expanded to require another pair of hands and Guy joined him as a partner. (Further expansion is taking place to enable them to produce up to 60 barrels per week).

In 1992 Dob's Best Bitter was a creditable third in the Great British Beer Festival (brewed for the Silverton Inn, who named it Dob's because they could not spell Dry Hopped Bitter). And the sheep? Well, they simply won't go away. The brewery has a supply of fresh spring water which it shares with a farmer up the road. When one day they ran out of water they were horrified to hear that their neighbour had used up all their water dipping his sheep! The Brewery currently produces four beers using only their fresh spring water, malt and hops with no additives. (The Exeter Old Bitter won the Strong Bitter Class at the 1993 Great British Beer Festival).

The beers are:

Exe Valley Bitter	1038°
Dob's Best Bitter	1041°
Devon Glory	1047°
Exeter Old Bitter	1047°

EXMOOR ALES

Golden Hill Brewery, Wiveliscombe, Somerset, TA4 2NY. Tel: 0984 23798

Exmoor Ales' own Jim Laker tells the story of how the brewery came to be in his hands, as one of city-slickers dropping out into the idyllic country from their stressed-out commercial life to become stressed-out brewers. Evidently, there was this cute little pub just outside a small sleepy town in Somerset called Wiveliscombe, where, despite the surliness of the landlord, his fine cellar skills attracted the less-sensitive locals. Two of them were recent fugitives from the horrors of big business, Pete Turner (an economist formerly with the company who recorded stars like Queen and David Bowie) and Jim Laker (a marketing man now enjoying rural peace and quiet as a smallholder/carpenter/part-time marketing consultant). Together they chatted and drank pints of the locally brewed Exmoor Ale. Jim was retained as a marketing consultant by the brewery who produced the beer and so was ready

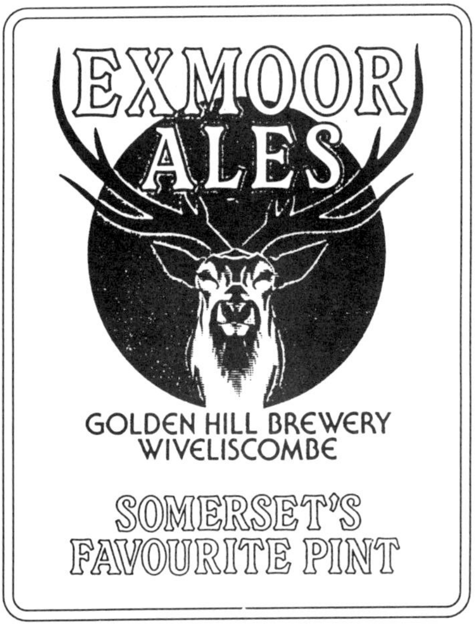

to talk Peter into helping him organise a management buy out when the original owner was ready to retire. As Jim says: 'We liked the beer so much, we bought the brewery(!)'.

As time went on, the countryside stayed idyllic, but the brewery rapidly developed into a madhouse, expanding, winning frequent awards for its beer and attracting top class staff such as Adrian Newman from 'a large brewery' north of the border. Despite their growth, the Exmoor-ites did not lose their sense of humour. Jim Laker is still considering 'Independence for Wiveliscombe' [accent on the third syllable] and can be found doing something unlikely every April Fool's Day to confuse the local radio station and amuse the Exmoor sheep. Meanwhile they concentrate on producing beer 'brewed by entirely traditional methods at Golden Hill Brewery using only West Country Malt and water which rises on the Brendon hills within Exmoor National Park'.

The beers are:

Exmoor Ale	1039°	
Exmoor Dark	1042°	(Occasional)
Exmoor Gold	1045°	
Exmoor Stag	1050°	
Exmoor Exmas	1058°	(in December)
Exmoor Beast	1066°	(brewed October to Easter.)

FOXLEY BREWING COMPANY

Unit 3, Homefarm Workshops, Mildenhall, Marlborough, Wilts, SN8 2LR.
Tel: 0672 515000

It was Rob Owen's academic thesis which persuaded him into brewing; that and the redundancy package which National Power provided for him and his partner, Neil Collings. As Rob looked into the background of the small brewing industry for his Diploma in Management Studies he came to realise that it was a feasible step for himself and Neil as they looked around for a new career. They moved into their industrial unit in August 1992, and started brewing a month later. The most vivid memories for Rob are the first brew (which they started late in the day and did not finish until six the next morning) and the help that breweries all around gave them during their first months. 'Everyone, both regional and other small breweries were really encouraging. They didn't mind us ringing up in panic because something had gone wrong, they had all experienced something similar (depending on their size) and were happy to give advice and practical help. We retrieve each other's barrels as well, which is a great benefit!' Although both Rob and Neil were keen home brewers, they had never attempted anything on a commercial scale before, but as Rob says 'at least it gives you somewhere to start from!' They learnt their brewing skills by learning from other brewers and ultimately by a bit of trial and error. It seems to be working now, however, because the brewery is expanding its capacity already. Which goes to show you can learn a lot from experience!

The beers are:

Foxley Best Bitter	1038°
Dog Booter	1046°/1048°

FREEMINER BREWERY

The Laurels, Sling, Coleford, Royal Forest of Dean. Tel: 0594 836 717

It cannot be said that many brewers get into brewing because they can't find any decent cider, but Don Burgess of the Freeminer Brewery claims just that. Don is an enthusiastic native of the Royal Forest of Dean and was horrified to find that in Manchester, where he studied for his degree cider was simply not up to his standard. He claims that his training was gained through dozens of Home-Brew Kits, but closer questioning reveals that he spent a formative fourteen months in Brendon Dobbins' West Coast Brewery in Manchester; he moved from one side of the bar to the other, almost immediately after he had graduated with his degree in microbiology. Moss Side in Manchester however, not surprisingly, did not have the same attraction as his own Royal Forest of Dean and Don soon decided that he was going to set up his own brewery. (As a Forester he says he can claim special ancient rights.) He said he missed the wild sheep wandering past his door in Manchester. Don, who is seriously thinking of setting up The Royal Forest of Dean Free State, is also fiercely independent about his beer. He will only use English hops and a traditional full mash. Since starting up in 1993, he currently produces 20 to 25 barrels per week which he mostly 'exports' round the country. Interestingly, the beer goes down particularly well in Manchester! His barrel identification system, he insists on telling people, is tricoloured – green for the trees of the Forest, black for the Coal and Brown for the Iron Ore (the Forest saw the very beginning of the Industrial Revolution).

In 1993, they took on their first tenancy, The Miners' Arms and are now specialising in beer-based cuisine and traditional ales and ciders. They have taken up the carpets and turned it back into a local pub, particularly useful for caving enthusiasts, whose muddy boots are not always welcome in more plush surroundings! Historical note: The Free Miners of the Royal Forest of Dean were awarded special privileges after they had helped out at the Battle of Bannockburn. They were mediaeval sappers and absolutely indispensable to any English King thinking of going to war.

The beers are:

Freeminer Bitter	1038°
Speculation Ale	1047°

GOACHERS BREWERY

Hayle Mill Cottages, Bockingford, Maidstone, Kent, ME15 6DJ.
Tel: 0622 682112

Phil Goacher and his wife gave themselves an anniversary present in 1992. To mark the tenth birthday of Goachers Brewery they bought themselves a pub. 'It's what we've always wanted – not a chain of pubs, just one to call our own'. This has been their ambition from the beginning and since moving to bigger premises they now own the freehold on their brewery – 'It's not a very exciting building, but like the pub it's ours!'

From his beginnings as a home brewer, he and his wife have built up a thriving 20 barrel a week business near Maidstone. They run the place between them, administration, delivery and, of course, brewing which is probably why Phil Goacher refers to himself as the head cook and bottlewasher. Over the years they have developed the range of beers in answer to popular demand. For instance, their lighter bitter was developed because of a run of hot summers a few years ago. They found the sales of their strong dark Maidstone Ale were suffering because drinkers wanted something lighter. So they developed their second light ale which really took off and is now their biggest seller.

They have always brewed a winter ale, but in 1992 they started a mild which has gone very well. The Goacher view is to give the public what they want, and it seems to have worked very well for them, since Phil says that he has never had to push the beers very heavily. 'They seem to sell by word of mouth'. At this rate they should start thinking about what they are going to give the brewery for its 21st anniversary!

The beers are:

Maidstone Real Mild	1033°
Maidstone Fine Light	1036°
Maidstone Best Dark	1040°
Maidstone Old 1066	1066°

GODDARD'S

Barnsley Farm, Bullen Road, Ryde, Isle of Wight, PO33 1QF. Tel: 0983 616833

If anything positive can be said to have come out of the recent troubles at Lloyds, Goddards Brewery could be one of them. Anthony Goddard, a Lloyds 'Name', had run his own vineyard on the Isle of Wight for some seventeen years when he was forced to sell up and move somewhere smaller. Looking around for a new business to go into, he had looked at buying and restarting the closed Burts Brewery on the Island. He is now pleased to say that the Receivers refused his offer but the process put him in touch with Jonathan Stansell, the Burts' head brewer. Anthony decided that his best option was to put a completely new 15 barrel length brewing plant into one of the buildings on his new property and start from scratch. They have only been brewing a few months but already reaction has been favourable to Goddard's Special Bitter.

Anthony, who is still a wine-maker at Barton Manor Vineyard on the island, leaves the brewing to Jonathan. He is discovering that brewing is a more complex process than wine-making, although he is appreciative of the fact that brewers do not have to grow their own raw materials, like winemakers, and the product is readier to sell far sooner! There are still of course many things in common, apart from producing an alcoholic drink; balance and cleanness of taste are paramount in both activities. Unfortunately, if you want to taste Goddard's Special Bitter you will have to travel to the Isle of Wight for the experience. The beer is not available on the mainland and there are no plans to 'export' in the near future.

The beer is:

Goddards Special Bitter	4%
Goddards Winter Warmer	5.2% approx

GUERNSEY BREWERY CO (1920) LTD

South Esplanade, St Peter Port, Guernsey, Channel Isles. Tel: 0481 720143

Guernsey Brewery has a very different story to most small independent brewers and can count its age in dozens of decades rather than months. Despite all this, unlike many brewers which were founded in the nineteenth century it still only produces under 200 barrels per week. Perhaps part of this is due to its belonging to Guernsey, also small and, of course, an island. Although the original family who set up the brewery no longer run it, it is still a very traditional business.

Directors work their way up through the ranks, with the present managing director John Shakerley having joined over thirty years ago as an assistant brewer. Perhaps a better flavour of the company can be seen in the determined way they kept going throughout the German occupation (despite some valuable members of staff, including the head brewer, being deported to Germany). Not only did they have to prove resourceful to combat the shortage of sugar and malt they also had to cope with their offices being turned into a hospital (including a mortuary in the garage). But their most innovative ideas came when they had to keep delivering their beer despite the ban on petrol for civilian purposes. Many traditional drays these days have horses pulling them, but probably nobody has ever seen a retired bull in the shafts. But necessity is the mother of invention and there is a splendid photograph of the dray complete with bovine traction unit!

The beers are:

Pony Ale	1037°
IPA	1045°
Best Bitter	1045°
Real Draught Bitter	1045°
LBA Mild	1037°
Stout	1039°
Brown	1038°

GUERNSEY BREWERY

La Couture Inn, La Couture, St. Peter Port, Guernsey.

HADRIAN BREWERY LTD

Unit 7, Foundry Lane Industrial Estate, Byker, Newcastle upon Tyne, NE6 1LH. Tel: 091 276 5302

Trevor Smith and his wife launched The Hadrian Brewery in 1987 and named it after the Roman Emperor who built a wall. Over the last few years, it must have seemed as though Trevor was trying to recreate the Roman Empire single-handed as he battled against banks, government departments and bureaucracy to keep his brewery afloat. Trevor had started like so many brewers as a lover of cask-conditioned ale and a believer in traditional values. He had looked into the idea of setting up on his own some years before 1987 but had decided that the time was not right. As it was, he took a year to plan what he was intending to do and as he said by the end of this time: 'It seemed like a good idea!' Over the first twelve months they were producing an average of six barrels per week. 'We weren't overworked, but then we weren't overpaid!', says Trevor. However, business increased steadily, and eventually they were looking around to expand. This was when the difficulties started.

For some reason, the bank would not lend them the £15,000 needed to increase their production by a modest figure, yet when they went in with a more ambitious plan which required £25,000 the bank welcomed them with open arms. They tripled production (and overheads) but unfortunately they also multiplied their number of bad debts, so as the business progressed the cash flow deteriorated and eventually there was simply not enough money to pay the Duty Bill to HM Customs and Excise. The bank then called in the Receivers and there was nearly a very unhappy ending to this tale. However, customers of the brewery, Michael and Wendy Westwell stepped in bought the brewery and kept Trevor on as a director in charge of brewing. 'We must have been doing something right', he commented. 'All the people who contacted the Receivers to buy the business were either customers or were trade connections and they all wanted me to stay on as brewer!' The business is now expanding healthily and looks set to see a good few years of success producing over 30 barrels per week and expanding.

The beers are:

Gladiator Bitter	1039°
Centurion Best Bitter	1045°
Emperor Ale	1050°

HAMBLETON ALES

The Brewery, Holme on Swale, Thirsk, North Yorks, YO7 4JE.
Tel: 0845 567460

Just fifty miles from his brother Martin at Dent brewery, Nick Stafford runs his Hambleton Ales brewery as living proof that he does know how to run a business. Since previous jobs as a headmaster and a computer software salesman have often involved furious rows with employers who have disagreed with his methods, Nick regards this as his vindication. Since the brewery has also increased his neckline, his waistline, and given him a slipped disc, the victory has not been without some physical effort! Over the past few years there have also been moments which have also taken their toll on Nick's peace of mind, such as the night the brewery roof fell in just before he went on holiday, which gave him a fortnight of worry. When he came back however he was delighted to learn that the brew which had been collapsed upon had not suffered at all in the tragedy – and was counted as one of the best ever!

The brewery is housed in an old Victorian brick-built barn in his in-laws' garden and Nick claims that it was seeing his brother producing excellent beer which convinced him that he could produce some that was at least as good if not better. The two brothers operate in friendly rivalry, both competing with and selling each other's beers. As Nick comments 'Fifty miles is just far enough away from each other!' Although only two years old, the brewery has increased its output by 100% (from 17 barrels to 35 barrels per week) and won champion beer at the Burton on Trent Beer Festival ('Second only to the Great British Beer Festival in prestige value' claims Nick). Finally, why have these two West country men moved to Yorkshire? 'We are adopted Northerners – once we had seen this part of the world we were determined to make it our home'.

The beers are:

Best Bitter	3.6%
Stallion	4.2%

HAMPSHIRE BREWERY

5 Anton Trading Estate, Andover, Hants. Tel: 0264 336699

Going on a brewing course is designed to give would-be brewers professional expertise. In the case of Steve Winduss and Simon Paine of the Hampshire Brewery it also gave them a business partner each! They had both worked in the drinks industry previously, and had both been enthusiastic and skilful home brewers, so they were obviously well-matched. They found themselves a soulless but very efficient industrial unit and started up in business. Neither Steve nor Simon think small, so they set up a 25 barrel brew-plant immediately (so that they could brew a reasonable amount in one go and then get on with the serious business of selling it!).

The beers are:

King Alfred Bitter*	1038°
Arthur Pendragon	1048°
Richard the Lionheart	1042°
William the Conqueror's	1066°
Hampshire Porter	1045°

*This got off to a good start by winning first prize at the Basingstoke Beer Festival.

HARVIESTOUN BREWERY

Dollar, Clackmannanshire, Central, FK14 7LX. Tel: 02594 2141

Ken Brooker is really a Dagenham man, so in his life before brewing it was natural for him to work for the biggest local business, the Ford Motor Company. When they sent him up to Scotland, he discovered that he really liked the place, so when Ford offered him a promotion down South again, he decided that he wanted to stay where he was. He had long been an ardent home brewer, producing over 20 gallons a week. Since he was already providing beer for all his friends and neighbours, it seemed an obvious next step to install a commercial plant, and make his living doing what he enjoyed most. He said goodbye to Ford, found himself premises in a 200 year old stone byre and assembled his first brew plant in 1984 out of vessels from a variety of sources. The business expanded and finally in 1992 he commissioned its replacement, a shiny new 20 barrel capacity installation. Over the years many things have happened which bring a smile to Ken's face and if you should meet him, ask what the time is. He may even tell you that he now has a watch which is waterproof to 100 metres – just in case he falls into the mash tun again and finds himself up to his ankles (from the head up) in warm hops and water. Ken managed to struggle out unharmed, but unfortunately, the watch could not take so much wort in one go!

The beers are:

Waverley 70/-	1037°
Original 80/-	1041°
Ptarmigan 85/-	1045°
Old Manor	1050°
Nouveau	(strength changes every year)

HOG'S BACK BREWERY

Manor Farm Business Park, The Street, Tongham, Surrey. Tel: 0252 782328

For quite a long time before they set up shop the Hunt family wanted to run a brewery. They had long been interested in traditional ale and had developed their expertise through years of home brewing and experimentation. They had also run a wholesaling business selling other brewers' beers and so were used to going around seeing how other brewers were operating and learning from their mistakes or from their good advice. All they needed was the financial investment. Luckily, they saw an advertisement in a magazine in which Anthony Stanton, a graphic design specialist sought a brewery to become involved with. Anthony became an honorary member of the Hunt family and a partner in the business. He is also the originator of all the art work for everything for the brewery from pump clips to tee-shirts. Ever resourceful, the Hog's Back also runs a regular brewery trip (every Wednesday evening at 6.30 pm (ring them to book yourself on to it – the trips are booked up months in advance). They have also recently started a special tour where they invite their publican customers to bring regulars along to see where the beer is made. They run a brewery shop which sells over 100 different bottled beers and an extensive range of English wines, particularly fruit wines plus cakes, pickles, mustards and all sorts of other produce made with beer.

The beers are:

Hogs Back Traditional English Ale (T.E.A.)	4.2%
Hogs Back Old Tongham Tasty (O.T.T.)	6.5%

HOOK NORTON BREWERY CO LTD

Hook Norton, Banbury Oxon, OX15 5NY. Tel: 0608 737210

To some extent the early success of the Hook Norton Brewery in Oxfordshire seemed to follow the development of the industrialisation of the area. From its beginnings in the middle of the nineteenth century when the young John Harris diversified from malting into brewing, it rapidly grew because of an expanding local demand. The navvies who were in the area for a long time building the railway and the local ironstone industry provided plenty of thirsty drinkers for Harris's beer, and it was not long before the brewery was undergoing its third expansion in less than 50 years. By 1900 a magnificent 'state of the art' tower brewery was being installed along with a splendid 25 horse power steam engine (which still does its job providing the power for pumps to lift water from the brewery's well and for pumping hot wort on the ground floor to the flat cooler on the fourth storey).

The tradition of the brewery still lives in the shape of David Clarke, a direct descendant of John Harris's nephew Alban who had been managing director before 1917. Hook Norton is different from most small independent brewers with its long history and its comparatively large estate of nearly 40 inns and taverns. But it is still independent and compared to the large regionals still very small. However, an indication of its enduring success can be seen in its availability on many supermarket shelves all over the country.

The beers are:

Hook Norton Mild	1032°
Hookey Best Bitter	1036°
Old Hookey	4.6°
Jackpot	3.4°
Hook Ale	3.0°

HOPBACK BREWERY

27 Estcourt Road, Salisbury, Wiltshire, SP1 3AS

John Gilbert and Roger McBride got together six years ago and decided to brew their own beer. They were not coming into the industry as enthusiastic amateurs. They had already been part of brewing industry for some time. John had worked for Watney's at Mortlake, in London and Roger had come from the Royal Tunbridge Wells brewery, among others. John says 'I just wanted to work for myself now. So I looked for the right pub and took it.' The right pub was the Wyndham Arms in Salisbury. They closed it for a few weeks for refurbishment, opened for business at Easter, and brewed their first pint in June. Right from the start they were successful. Their Special was awarded a Highly Commended at the Great British Beer Festival in its first year and they were given the accolade of Best New Brewery four years ago. Their Summer Lightning has won over twenty prizes over the last few years, achieving the heights of Best Strong Beer at the Great British Beer Festival in 1992. Hopback have grown enormously since their early days. They now have two pubs and two breweries. They're producing over eighty barrels a week and employ eight full time members of staff.

The beers are:

Mild	1032°
GFB	1035°
Special	1041°
Wilt Alternative	1041°
Stout	1043°
Summer Lightning	1050°
Wheat Beer	1050°

HULL BREWERY

144-148 English Street, Hull, N. Humberside, HU3 2BT. Tel: 0482 586364/5

Once upon a time there was a brewery in Hull which owned 300 pubs. Unfortunately, it was bought out by a bigger brewery and they closed it down. However, along came along a fairy godperson who wanted to start it all up again. He asked Peter Austin to build the brewery for him and Peter recommended Dennis Armstrong to help run it. They first started brewing in 1989. Since then one of the original partners has retired to run one of the new brewery's pubs and the business is in Dennis's capable hands. He has over twenty years of experience in the drinks industry, having been both a publican and a training manager for one of the national brewers. Paul Wardropper is the Head Brewer.

True to Hull's fishing tradition, the brewery is housed in an old curing house (which no longer smells of kippers!) and they own a pub just off the old dockside. The plant now brews between 45 and 50 barrels per week. Dennis comments: 'It has been a very exciting time to start a brewery – the Monopolies and Mergers Commission has not really helped new breweries, but we felt that if we had not started it when we did, we might have missed the boat. The recession has not helped but we have had an exciting, not to say worrying time over the last few years – but we now employ nine people and we're getting bigger so we must have made the right decision!'

The beers are:

Mild	1033°
Bitter	1036°
Guvernor	1048°

JUDGES

Church Lawford Business Centre, Limestone Hall Road, Church Lawford, Warwickshire. Tel: 0788569831

Mayday 1992 marked a day of freedom for Geoff and Anne Judge. After 25 years as an accountant, Geoff decided that 20% job satisfaction from his job as financial director of a group of companies was simply not enough. Anne agreed and they decided to hand in their notices without a clue about what they were going to do next, except that it would be something they enjoyed. A conversation with his friend, the licensee of the local free house set Geoff on the road to his brewery and four months after they started looking, suitable premises presented themselves and the brewery was under way. Ever enterprising, they bought and fitted their own plant even down to welding the stainless steel themselves. Two weeks of training and a couple of visits from a brewing consultant later and Geoff decided that it was time that he and Anne stood on their own four feet. After five months of 'nearly every mistake you could think of making' the hard work paid off. The beer became consistent (to the extent of winning three prizes at the local Rugby Beer Festival) and Geoff is pleased to say that it 'sells itself'. Right at the beginning they had decided they would keep the business 'in the family' and that Geoff would get to know all his publican customers. He now offers a seven-day-per-week service and every barrel is still delivered by Geoff personally.

The beers are:

Gavel Bender	1050°
Barristers Bitter	1038°
Santa's Surprise	1052° (Christmas)

KELHAM ISLAND BREWERY

23 Alma Street, Sheffield, S3 8SA. Tel: 0742 728195

The day the Monopolies and Mergers Commission reported on the Brewing Industry, Dave Wicket was sitting in his office at Sheffield Polytechnic and decided 'Now I am going to build a brewery and sell my beer to other pubs as guest ales.' He had already bought a pub called The Fat Cat and immediately started applying for planning permission to build his brewhouse in the back yard. He went off to Oxford to buy a brewplant from a brewpub that had closed down and then had to store it until he had constructed the building to go round it. He told his wife 'I will have a brewery over here, and a pub in America within the next two years' and promptly gave up his job as a Lecturer in Business Studies. True to his promise, he had achieved both his ambitions before the year was out (and is now being invited back to Sheffield Hallam University, as it is now called, to give occasional lectures on their brewing courses). His staff were equally precipitous about starting their careers with Dave.

His brewer, Patrick Malcolm threw up his job as an engineer to learn to brew at Kelham Island (a district in Sheffield) and the other member of staff came over from Montreal for a month and never went home. It is no wonder that Dave describes his brewery as having 'a happy atmosphere' although this may also be because they are so successful that they are now bursting out of their original building and looking for new premises. The beer they brew has no additives (not even sugar) and Dave's greatest joy is that he can experiment as and how he wants with the beer. They currently brew around 12 barrels per week, but when they move premises this will increase. Dave Wicket is also memorable as the man who tried to buy an entire redundant brewery from Whitbread.

The beers are:

Pale Rider	4.8%	(A wheat beer made with 100% American hops)
Cherry Beer	5.7%	
Kelham Island Bitter	5.5%	
Celebration Bitter	1046°	

KEMPTOWN BREWERY COMPANY LTD

The Hand in Hand, 33 Upper Street, James's Street, Kemptown, Brighton, BN2 1JN. Tel: 0273 699595

To say that Bev Robin's career in brewing started as a joke would not be entirely true, but a chance conversation at the Great British Beer Festival in Leeds in 1988 set in motion a train of events which ended with the resurrection of the name of the Kemptown Brewery Company, which had closed down some 25 years before. Bev himself has spent most of his working life in the licensed trade, having been (he says) weaned on cider. He started his home brew activities at the age of 14 ('in the days before these easy-to-use kits') and has since risen to become not

From a Kemptown Brewery Christmas card

only a local publican and brewer but also chairman of the local Licensed Victuallers Association, the trade body which represents publicans all over the country. So when the suggestion to turn the empty space behind Bev's Hand in Hand pub in Brighton was made, after thinking about it, he thought it was a good idea (although he was going into expansion at the beginning of a recession!) Suitable brewery plant was found from all over the country and had to be craned into position. Bev and his friends then set about building the brewery around the plant, with the copper taking pride of place in what had originally been a bathroom.

The first pint was brewed in November 1989 over a year after the idea was conceived. No birth, of course, is ever without some difficulty and early disputes with the water authority (which involved digging umpteen holes all around the pub) were eventually resolved (it only took nine months!) Another mistake at the beginning was the double helping of malt in the first brew of Bev's winter ale, Old Grumpy, which resulted in a much stronger beer than originally intended. However, the success of the 'mistake' was such that Bev had to try and remember how he did it, and has carried on with it ever since.

The beers are:

Kemptown Mild	1036°
Budget Bitter	1036°
Kemptown Bitter	1040°
Celebrated Staggering Ale	1050°
Staggering in the Dark (SID)	1052°
Old Grumpy	1062°

LAKELAND BREWERY COMPANY

Strawberry Bank, Cartmel Fell, Grange over Sands, Cumbria, LA11 6NW.
Tel: 044 88486

Nigel and Helen Stevenson had been in their pub at Strawberry Bank in Cumbria for eleven years before they decided to set up their own brewery. They had always stocked a range in excess of 200 different beers from all over the world, so they considered making a Lakeland brew would fit the last piece in the jigsaw. The view from the front terrace of the pub is a dramatic valley and the Stevensons made the most of the area's association with writer Arthur Ransome (remember Swallows and Amazons?) when they named their beers. If asked about his own background, Stevenson is much enthusiastic about the author and is keen to tell you how he was the last journalist to escape from Moscow during the 1917 Revolution and how he came to settle in the village with Trotsky's secretary. (If you're lucky you might even meet one of the locals in the pub who still remembers Ransome as a neighbour.)

The beers are:

Amazon Bitter	4%	'Swallow an Amazon' goes the slogan
Great Northern	5%	
Big Six	6%	Named after one of Ransome's books
Damson Beer	7%	Made with local Lyth Valley damsons
Knickerbocker Breaker		A scrumpy cider which uses apples from local farmers.

LARKINS

Chiddingstone, Eden Bridge, Kent, TN8 7BB. Tel: 0892 870328

The Dockerties have been farming in East Sussex and Kent for hundreds of years. Marjorie remembers when some years ago, the family made the decision to leave dairy farming. They were looking around for something else to do now that the cattle had gone and, as the Royal Tunbridge Wells Brewery had shut down, bought the equipment and had it installed on their Larkins farm in Eden Bridge. They took on the brewer from the old brewery, but he was close to retirement and it was not long before their son Bob, who was already an enthusiastic home brewer and something of a chemist, took over. They recall how in the early days, in 1986, they had to go and find their customers one by one, and are pleased with the way the small independent brewery industry has gone. 'People now seek out our beers, rather than us trying to find them', Marjorie was pleased to report.

Is there any connection between the H.E. Bates family of Larkins and the brewery? Larkins Farm apparently was owned by two brothers Theobald and Bartholomew Lovikins in the 12th Century (a long time before the TV series!) and the name evolved over the years. 'And anyway', says Marjorie, 'they say Puffick! (not Perfick) in these parts when they mean perfect'. But they did strike a blow for the individual when the TV company put 'Kentish Ales' on some bottles of promotional beer – because Larkins own the name. 'They were apologetic and have given us some good publicity,' say Larkins, 'but we wonder how generous they would have been if the fault had been the other way round?'

The beers are:

Traditional Bitter	1035°
Sovereign Bitter	1040°
Best Bitter	1045°
Porter Ale	1055°

LINFITT BREWERY

The Sair Inn, Lane Top, Lynthwaite, Huddersfield, Yorks, HD7 5SG.
Tel: 0484 842370

Jane and Ron Crabtree never intended setting up a brewery in the Sair Inn near Huddersfield. For one thing they already had a brewery somewhere else. They had only bought the pub as an outlet for their beers. However, Ron and his partner in the brewery parted company and the Crabtrees found they had no alternative but to brew their own. Over the years the business has developed (with some minor hiccoughs) and their range has grown from one beer to eight. They brew around eight barrels per week but production was hampered in 1993 by Ron having to take time from his brewing to develop his new pub-brewery kit, designed 'to cost hundreds of pounds rather than thousands' to enable other pubs to start brewing.

When a pub buys Ron's kit, at least they will know the designer has gone through all the problems they are likely to meet (plus maybe a few more). Ron, for instance, remembers the time when Jane went out shopping leaving him to do the brewing and found him trying to rescue a fermenting vessel full of beer which he had stripped down to cure a blocked pipe. He says that Jane 'came in and found me laughing hysterically, running up and down a ladder with a bucket, trying to pour beer that was flowing out of the bottom back into the top.' He only lost a quarter of the beer, he says, 'but a lot of weight!'

The beers are:

Mild	1032°
Bitter	1035°
Special	1041°
English Guineas Stout	1050°
Old Eli	1050°
Leadboiler	1063°
Enoch's Hammer	1080°
Xmas Ale	1082°

LITTLE AVENHAM BREWERY

Gaston's Real Ale and Fine Wine Pub, 30 Avenham Street, Preston, Lancs.
Tel: 0772 556900

Unlike many small independent brewers, the drinks trade was nothing new to David Bell when he decided to make his own beer. His family had been in the industry for many years and the new venture was an addition to a business which includes a country hotel and a thriving wholesale business. The brewery is behind Gaston's Wine Bar in Preston and the brewing is done by the licensee David Murray. This is another brewery which has a strong sense of local involvement. Not only do they name their beers in line with local customs, they also make a point of brewing with wild hops which grow on the hedgerows in the countryside around Preston. Appropriately called Hedgerow Bitter, they have a waiting list of Fylde pubs eager to take the beer, even though output is tiny. One problem last season was that when the volunteers went out last season to collect the hops, sometimes the trimmers had got there before them – so if any local farmers are beer enthusiasts, let David know when you are about to cut your hedges!

The beers are:

Pickled Priest	1036°	Preston was originally known as Priest's Town
Clog Dancer	1038°	Named after a competition in the pub – beer is known locally as 'wallop', and so is a clog
Torchlight	1050°	Preston Guild holds a special torch-lit procession every twenty years, and this beer was first brewed in a 'Guild Year'
Pierrepoint's Last Drop	1064°	The last public executioner (named Pierrepoint) was a local licensee. 'It's a killer', commented David.

LLOYDS COUNTRY BEERS

John Thompson Inn, Ingleby, Derbyshire. Tel: 0332 863426

In the late 1970s Chris Voyce was fed up with his temporary job at Marston's Brewery, so he answered an advert in his local paper for a general dogsbody. It wasn't until he arrived that he realised it was a brewery, owned by Colin Lloyd (hence the name). After about a month Colin went on holiday leaving Chris in charge after a quick training session. Chris was really on his own now, because not understanding his boss's name mis-pronounced by the Portuguese telephone operator he refused to take a reverse charge call. It all worked out eventually of course, with Chris buying the business in 1983 to become the only independent brewery in Derbyshire.

Fame spread rapidly so that as well as his regular beers, Chris was brewing a regular festival ale for the Nottingham branch of CAMRA and a very special beer for the Lord Mayor of Nottingham. The brewery is now averaging 20 barrels per week with peaks of 30 barrels a week in the summer. Chris reckons that it was inevitable that he would end up a brewer – his grandfather was a licensee and his father worked for a company which collected brewers' grains, and he eventually came to live in the brewing industry's Mecca, Burton on Trent, because his parents lived there. For those people not able to make a formal visit to the brewery, but who happen to be flying into East Midlands Airport, Chris recommends that you look out of the window just before you land. If you see a white building with a big St George's Cross flag flying – you've seen the brewery!

The beers are:

Derby Mild	1033°
Lloyds Classic	1035/38°
Derby Bitter	1042°
VIP	1048°
Porter	1067°
Christmas Skullcrusher	1067°

McGuinness:

see *Thomas McGuiness Brewing Co.*

MALTON BREWERY COMPANY

Crown Hotel, Wheelgate, Malton, N. Yorks, YO17 0HP

Geoff Woollons at The Malton Brewery Company must take pride of place as a senior member of the small independent brewing movement. He has been in the industry ever since he left school over forty-five years ago, and has worked for many famous (but now alas defunct) breweries such as the Russell Brewery and Charles Rose. He was also head brewer at Mitchells and Butler's Highgate Brewery. But he had always wanted to bring brewing back to his hometown of Malton and so when the opportunity to take early retirement came his way in 1982 it gave him the opportunity to build a small brewery behind his brother-in-law's pub in Wheelgate, Malton.

Originally, the brewery was 'just something to do', but it was not long before other people realised that he was producing extremely good beer. Nowadays, not only does he sell to local pubs and through a few agencies, but customers have been known to come from Chelmsford, Leicester and Lancashire to pick up supplies. Of course, he also has a fund of knowledge about brewing which he uses to encourage healthy competition in the industry. He has already helped provide training for other well-known brewers such as John Constable at Butterknowle, the Stafford Brothers (Hambleton and Dent Breweries) and Geoff Hirst at Hardingham.

Whether these youngsters have the energy that Geoff shows at his age of 68 only time will tell. He's up at 3.00 a.m. two or three mornings a week with his assistant Colin Sykes to brew 'because I'm used to it!'

The beers are:

Pale Ale	1034°	
Double Chance Bitter	1038°	named after the Grand National winner which was stabled in the stable block that later became the brewery.
Pickwick's Porter	1042°	
Owd Bob	1055°	

MAULDON'S BREWERY

7 Addison Road, Chilton Industrial Estate, Sudbury, Suffolk, CO10 6YW.
Tel: 0787 311055

Perhaps a brewery whose origins go back to 1795 could not be called one of the 'new wave'. However, since the original firm ceased trading earlier this century, and a descendant of the original family, Peter Mauldon, wanted to resurrect the name, it does come under the category of a new business. Peter himself has been in the brewing industry all his life. He has worked with one of the nationals in huge plants all over the country, so the skills needed to set up the new venture were already in place. Unfortunately, everything else had to be bought in.

He acquired the 'uncharismatic' building in September 1982 and by December 1982 he had put some plant together and had started brewing. The new 'old' brewery caused a ripple of interest among locals, with TV and newspapers giving them good coverage. Some pubs even rang up asking if they could be 'the first' to take the new brews, but things grew fairly steadily until the moment in August 1991 when their strong porter, Blackadder won the Champion Beer at the Great British Beer Festival. Since then, they have been famous the length and breadth of the land! The story of the development and the name are typical of small brewery ventures – hard work, a little luck and an imaginative way of looking at things are essential ingredients to success.

Blackadder was originally a special order for a pub who wanted a strong version of the Mauldon standard porter. It went down so well, that it was decided to brew it on a larger basis for general consumption. The name came from a standard Mauldon Brewery practice of encouraging pubs to think up a name with a free nine-gallon cask as the prize for the winning entry. Blackadder came up and was considered a very apt description of the 1055° beer. It was only later that it was discovered how apt it was for the brewery. It seemed that in 1771 in the village of Acton, where the brewery is based, the gentleman who owned the place sold a house to someone called James Blackadder. So it was truly a stroke of luck that the name of their most celebrated beer actually predates even the original brewery and is based on a character so close to home (and gains publicity from reruns of the popular TV series). Unfortunately the Blackadders are no longer around in the Suffolk village, but their memory lingers on!

The beers are:

Golden Brew	1034°
Bitter	1037°
Old Porter	1042°
Old XXXX	1042°
Squires	1044°
Special	1045°
Suffolk Punch	1050°
Black Adder	1055°
Christmas Reserve	1065°
Suffolk Comfort	1065°

THE MILL BREWERY

Unit 18C Hanbury Buildings, Bradley Lane, Newton Abbot, S. Devon. TQ12 1LZ. Tel: 0626 63322

The Mill Brewery was the result of a particularly disappointing stag night. Dave Hedge and his friend Paul Bigrig were both so dissatisfied at the quality of the beer in 1982 in their part of Devon that they decided they could do better themselves. However, both decided that they would not give up their day jobs, and still pursue their separate careers as an independent financial consultant and a professional engineer respectively. How do they fit it all in? 'With difficulty and very long hours', said Dave.

Amazingly enough, they produce between 5 and 12 barrels per week between them with no outside help. Of the incidents which have happened to them over the last 11 years, they most vividly remember the day when they gave a bath to a bunch of lads who had just completed a charity pub crawl – somewhat the worse for wear. Dave simply heated up some water in the mash tun and let them get on with it! They also remember the difficulty they had naming their beers, and how after going through the process of setting up a competition for the best one, they eventually ended making a final decision just as they were about to go on air with the local radio station. They finally chose to call their beers after the popular word for a Devonian – Janner.

The beers are:

Janners Ale	1038°
Janners Old Original	1045°
Janners Christmas Ale	1050°

MOLES BREWERY

(Cascade Drinks) 5 Merlin Way, Bowerhill, Melksham, Wilts. SN12 6TJ. Tel: 0225 708842

Eleven years ago the owner of a soft drinks company wanted to start a brewery, but did not know how. Luckily for him, his next door neighbour remembered a friend from college who had gone on to take an apprenticeship at Usher's Brewery in Trow-

bridge. The soft drinks manufacturer and the old college chum were introduced and thus it was that Roger Catte, after a string of lucky coincidences came to start a brewery from scratch. He called it 'Mole's' after his own nickname. Eventually, Roger bought not only the brewery but the whole business from the original owner and now runs the company with the help of 18 other people. He says 'I had to buy the company – I think I am unemployable by anyone but myself!'. He brews between 30 and 50 barrels per week, and some of this goes to his own small chain of twelve pubs, which he has purchased on lease from a large brewery. 'It's a hell of a risk' he says 'but we have to guarantee a market for ourselves, and the best way to do it is with our own pubs. The large brewers are punishing the small ones worse than ever before the beer orders and some of the discounts that the big companies are offering to publicans exclude us from even attempting to compete.'

The beers are:

Tap Bitter	1035°
Best Bitter	1040°
Brew 97	1050°
XB	1060°
Own Ale	1038°
Guvnor's Special Brew	1048°

MOORHOUSES BREWERY CO

Moorhouse Street, Burnley, Lancs. B11 5EN. Tel: 0282 422864

Malcolm MacDonald began his working life as a manager in the light engineering industry. But his family has connections with the brewing industry and it was not long before he was managing a Whitbread pub. He did this for five years until he was approached by a member of his family who had just acquired Moorhouses. In the best entrepreneurial tradition, the new owner had been so impressed by the quality of the pint of beer he tasted in a pub outside Preston that he simply had to buy the brewery. This was in 1985 and the business ticked over until 1987 when Malcolm stepped in to galvanize it into life. The output went up from 30 barrels per week to 150 and the turnover increased dramatically. The old building (dating from 1870 – but too ugly to be a national treasure) is now bursting at the seams and expansion to a new site is planned in the near future.

Apparently in the nineteenth century Moorhouses was famous for its non-intoxicating drinks. Malcolm is pleased to say that this is no longer the case – it is their beer that makes them a local household name!

The beers are:

Black Cat Mild	1034°
Premier Bitter	1036°
Pendle Witches Brew	1050°
Owd Ale	1065°

MUNDANE ALES

38 Outwoods Street, Burton on Trent, Staffs, DE14 2PJ. Tel: 0283 67173

Don't believe everything that you read – Bob Dummons believes that his beers are anything but mundane. 'But everybody else had used all the superlatives – so we thought we would be a bit tongue-in-cheek'. Bob's business has grown organically – everything has developed quite naturally from within since the Dummons bought their pub in 1987. After 21 years with British Telecom, Bob took over the Waggon and Horses in Halesowen, and immediately set about getting in as big a variety of beers as he could. Once, he was in partnership with Lloyds Country Beers, and got used to driving all over the country to pick up beers from different breweries for his own pub. This naturally led to some breweries asking him to pick up beers from other people for their own pubs and the wholesale side of the business was born. 'It came at a good time', admits Bob. 'I'd been a licensee before and I needed an extra challenge'. But perhaps the ultimate challenge was the brewery. He had long been a full mash home brewer and the opportunity to buy the old Keystone Brewery equipment and set up in a listed cooperage saw mill was irresistible.

The first beer is:

Opening Medicine 1040° (more to follow)

NETHERGATE BREWERY LTD

11-13 High Street, Clare, Suffolk, CL10 8NY. Tel: 0787 277244

Ian Hornsey and Dick Burge had been talking about setting up their own brewery for years. They came from very different walks of life, (Ian is a Ph.D. former academic lecturer and Dick once owned his own petrol company) although they had been to school together. As well as his scientific knowledge, Ian gained practical experience by helping out as unpaid relief brewer for a regional brewery. His students must have counted themselves very lucky when their industrial experience visits took them to breweries! Eventually the talking came to fruition and Nethergate was set up in 1985 in the historic village of Clare in Suffolk, alongside the Nethergate Wine Company. Ian with his flowing beard and pipe looks like everybody's idea of a traditional brewer and when he talks about his recipes and his strict adherence to his own very high standards, he sounds like one as well. 'I believe every beer should have its own recipe (we have two brews based on two different 18th century recipes and one on an old Halifax recipe). I also believe in only using English hops and I will not accept malt which is not to my own specification'. But Ian also has the touch of the forgetful professor about him which has led to some funny incidents – including the time his shirt went all round the world without him and the day his assistant brewer found him hanging on by his feet in the mash tun.

The brewery is a great success – they have recently trebled their capacity and Ian remembers the day when they had to brew a second lot of Christmas ale before Christmas because the first batch had sold out so quickly. Once of their products is so successful – Nethergate Old Growler in bottles can be found on supermarket shelves – that they have to rent MacMullen's brew-house to brew enough to satisfy their customers. However, Ian hastens to add that it is only MacMullen's equipment that is used – all the expertise is his!

The beers are:

IPA	1036°
Bitter	1039°
Old Growler	1054°

NEW INN, CROPTON BREWERY

The New Inn, Cropton, Pickering, N. Yorks. Tel: 0751 5330

The New Inn in Cropton, an old coaching hostelry, which still sticks to the old rules of providing any weary traveller with water and bread to refresh them, can offer the discerning voyager something much more enticing these days. Since 1984 it has been steadily growing its reputation for the beer that is brewed on the premises. When the then owner of the New Inn decided to brew ale, it was strictly for his own customers. When Michael Lee took over the pub two years later he decided that he was going to sell the beer to other publicans. Since then, the two-barrel plant has expanded to ten-barrels, and there are plans for yet more expansion on the way since it is now operating at full capacity.

The brewery has also commemorated one of Cropton village's most famous sons in their Scoresby Stout, named after Captain Scoresby, a fearless and prolific whaler of the nineteenth century (in the days of Moby Dick when whaling was more acceptable). Captain Scoresby operated out of Whitby on the Yorkshire Coast. So famous was this gentleman that he had a stretch of Scandinavian waterway named after him, and now he has achieved ultimate immortality in having a stout named after him. Just like Captain Scoresby, Michael Lee's beer has travelled all round the country and when they have planning permission for the new brewery it looks set to travel further.

The beers are:

King Billy	1036/7°
Two Pints Best Bitter	1040/42°
Special Strong	1060°
Scoresby Stout	1044°

OAKHILL

Old Brewery, High Street, Oakhill, Bath, BA3 5AS. Tel: 0749 840134

Back in 1983 farmer Reg Keevil, seeing that the European Community were not about to do farmers any favours decided that he needed a guaranteed outlet for his barley, so he decided to set up a brewery. Those of you who know anything about malting barley for brewing will know that it simply is not that easy, so it was no surprise that Reg still does not provide the barley for his brews. However, ten years later the brewery is still there in its historic building. It is housed in the old Oakhill brewery which dates back to 1767 and is soon to expand to the maltings which once belonged to the old brewery. Reg is, of course, a farmer and, as such, is busy looking after his 1200 acres, plus his engineering business and a couple of pubs which he owns in the district. When he first started looking at the idea of starting a brewery, he was lucky to be able not only to buy the plant from the Beacon Brewery which was about to close, but also to call on the expertise of Jerry Watts, the owner who came to work for him. For the last four years the brewing has been done by John Lawton, also from an agricultural background, who had started brewing with Ringwood and David Bruce's Firkin pubs before joining Reg at Oakhill.

The beers are:

Oakhill Bitter	1044°
Yeoman's Strong Ale	1049°
Black Magic Stout	1044°

They also brew a summer Somer Ale (3.5%) and every year they provide Glastonbury Festival with a special brew.

ORIGINAL LION'S BREWERY

Griffin Brewery, Belshaw Court, Billington Road, Burnley, Lancs, BB1 5UB. Tel: 0282 830156

Jim Botur has been in brewing for nearly thirty years. He worked for Matthew Brown until they were taken over by Scottish and Newcastle. As a result the brewery in which Jim occupied a very senior position was closed down in 1991. As he says 'The only thing I knew was brewing.' So he immediately looked around for a way to continue on his own. He found himself some 'sleeping partners' who provided the money and set about building his own brewery, which he achieved in less than two months, using second-hand equipment and all his expertise as a brewer. He even managed to bring some ready-made staff with him in the shape of Ross Bamber as his head brewer.

The plant produces 40 to 50 barrels per week. Jim was determined to continue the tradition of the Lion ales that had been produced for so long in Blackburn, but he had problems because Scottish and Newcastle still owned the rights to the brand names. So Jim's beers are merely called Bitter and Mild on the pump clip, with the name of the brewery emblazoned over them. What appears to really motivate Jim is his annoyance at the Beer Orders which looked like they were going to spell greater choice and freedom for small independent brewer and customer, and which Jim thinks (along with many others) have gone so severely wrong that the big brewers now have even more of a stronghold than they used to. But, as he says, at least he's doing his bit to give them some competition!

The beers are:

Original Bitter	1038°
Owd Edgar	1068°

THE ORKNEY BREWERY

Quoyloo, Sandwick, Orkney, KW16 3LT. Tel: 0856 84802

Irene and Roger White have everything. They live on a remote island in the Orkneys, and to match the fairy-tale scenery, they met and married a few years ago in a whirlwind romance. 'I met Roger on the 6th August', said Irene, 'and he proposed on the 8th – I wondered what had taken him so long!'.

Roger, a teetotaller, started the brewery in a converted schoolhouse in April 1988 after a career which had spanned civil engineering (building multi-story car parks in the Middle East) and running a pub in Gloucester (He once put up a sign outside the pub declaring 'Free Beer Tomorrow' – when the locals came in demanding their free pints he reminded them the sign said 'tomorrow' – but since they were they might as well have a drink!)

Irene, on the other hand, had been an assistant head-teacher in Aberdeen and gladly abandoned her secure career to follow Roger's dream. How did he decide to start up as a brewer? 'I was lying on a beach somewhere out East' he recalls 'and realised that I had to do something with the rest of my life – so I opted for the most civilised place on earth – no roundabouts, no crime, and certainly no multi-storey car-parks!' Orkney's nearest brewery is 400 miles away, the whole county only boasts 18,000 people and most of their beer travels by boat to the mainland to be sold all over the British Isles, including far-distant Cornwall. The Whites along with head brewer, Alan Irvin and assistant Luke Kendall brew some 50 barrels per week and are proud that they were the first Scottish brewery to be represented in the Great British Beer Festival final.

RAVEN ALES

The beers are:

Raven Ale	1038°	
Dark Island	1045°	
Dragon Head Stout	1040°	
Skull Splitter	1080°	(named after Thorfinn, the seventh Viking Earl of Orkney who lived around 970 AD and had some fairly anti-social habits)

OTTER BREWERY LTD

Maythayes, Luppitt, Honiton, S. Devon, EX14 0SA. Tel: 0404 891 285

In 1982 Whitbread made brewer David McCaig redundant. By 1990 he thought it might be a good idea to get back into the brewing industry. As luck would have it next to his house in Devon there was a disused barn which could be converted into a brewery. So after a great deal of physical labour helping with the building work and even more mental effort, battling through the mounds of red tape the Otter Brewery was born in November of that year. 1991 was excellent, but a succession of disasters in the next year, starting with being supplied the wrong yeast, meant that only during 1993 have they been able to build up their reputation and again become 'flavour of the month'. David now cultivates his own yeast to avoid any further mistakes, and has reported his beer travelling throughout the country. Having just recovered from their initial building works David is once again putting his shoulder to the hod and contemplating moving the brewery round so that they can expand their production. They currently produce about 20 barrels per week.

The beers are:

Otter Head	5.8%	
Otter Ale	1044°	4.5%
Otter Bitter	1036°	3.6%

THE PILGRIM BREWERY

West Street, Reigate, Surrey, RH2 9BL. Tel: 0737 222651

They say that small breweries are often run by two men and a dog. This is indeed true of The Pilgrim Brewery in London commuter belt Reigate. The dog is a vital member of the team. In theory of course the brains behind the brewhouse is Dave Roberts, former Welsh Office and Ministry of Defence Civil Servant, who swapped the hushed corridors of Whitehall for his establishment on a tiny industrial estate behind a hairdresser and a sports shop in the busy town centre. Dave decided that brewing was for him when 'It got to a stage where I realised I was no longer in control of my own life.' he explains. 'I hated commuting and I had always been fascinated by people, brewing and pubs. My family includes publicans on one side, and bakers on the other – so there has always been a connection with yeast and beer! I wanted to go into business on my own and my father came back from a holiday in Devon where he had got drunk with the original owner of the Blackawton Brewery, one of the first micros – and that was it. It still took another couple of years to raise the money but in 1981 I started up on my own. The infant Pilgrim Brewery soon outgrew its tiny premises and I moved to Reigate in 1985. '

And what about the dog? Ah yes, don't visit the Pilgrim brewery if you're a sales representative. Otherwise Breeze, a black and white collie with a very curious arrangement of ears, who defends the property with more enthusiasm than efficiency, may well decide that you have business elsewhere. If however, you just want to buy some beer she will happily leave you to your conversation with Dave, while digging for bones on the local cricket pitch or pursuing her ball at furious speed round the yard. She must be of the few members of brewery management teams not allowed inside their brewery!

The beers are:

SPA	1037°
Porter	1041°
Progress Best Bitter	1041°
Crusader Premium Bitter	1047°
Saracen Stout	1047°
Talisman	1049°

PLASSEY BREWERY

Eyton, Wrexham, Clwyd, LL13 0SP. Tel: 0978 780922

Plassey Brewery was founded by Alan Beresford in 1985. Alan had previously been a brewer with Border Breweries in Wrexham for 20 years and when Marstons took over and closed the Brewery he decided to start his own in partnership with Tony Brookshaw, the owner of the 250 acre Plassey estate. The brewery was set up in an award winning Edwardian Shippon which has since developed to also house various craft centres, a restaurant and a Scandinavian Health Centre. Unfortunately in November 1989, Alan died after just having delivered ale to the Bridge Inn, in Pont Glyddyn. It was at this point when Tony Brookshaw approached Ian Dale to take over the brewery. Ian, who had been a close friend of Alan, had also spent ten years brewing with Border Breweries before Marstons closed it down. Ian at the time was a brewer at Wrexham Lager Brewery, and decided to take on the Plassey Brewery in his spare time. Ian declares, 'This has proved to be a very rewarding experience, brewing real ales to one's own taste as opposed to brewing national brand lagers.'

Since Ian has taken over, another two beers have been developed to complement the Plassey Bitter. The Plassey site has more to offer than just a brewery, with a towing caravan park and a new golf course. The Plassey beers prove very popular in the three bars on the site, which means there is little left over for sale outside as present capacity is limited. But there are plans for the brewery to enable them to expand both in terms of barrelage and range.

The beers are:

Plassey Bitter	1038°
Cwrw Tudn	1047°
Dragon Breath	1060°

REBELLION BEER COMPANY

The Marlow Brewery, Unit J, Rose Ind. Estate, Marlow Bottom Road, Marlow, Bucks, SL7 3ND. Tel: 0628 476594

Mark Gloynes was brought up in Marlow, Buckinghamshire, and went to school successively on both sides of the old Wethered's Brewery in that town. Perhaps it was this which kept bringing him back to the brewing industry through a university course in chemical engineering and even a high powered Master in Business Administration at the internationally respected Cranfield Business School. Every holiday he would try and get himself a temporary job in a brewery and eventually ended up in the next best thing, wineries in Australia, New Zealand and France. But, the call proved too great and he left off working for large international companies and went off to do his MBA to learn as much as possible about business before setting up on his own. His ideas were so good that his final project won the prize for the best business plan of the year, which of course happened to be the business plan for a small brewery! (Despite the prize being awarded by a large bank, the same bank refused to lend him the money when he went to his local branch with his scheme) However, he had already bought himself some plant which he kept in storage until he was ready and the day finally came when he could open the doors of the Rebellion brewery in his hometown of Marlow.

Although the brewery is presently in an industrial estate there are tentative plans afoot to move back into the old Wethereds brewery as part of a large city-centre regeneration project. Mark says "The old eighteenth century brewhouse is an attractive building and townspeople would like to see it as a focal point again as it once was when it was a large brewery. Even if we don't move into the brewhouse itself, we still see ourselves as a catalyst to get this project off the ground." After only a few months, Rebellion is brewing some eight barrels per week, but has a capacity for around 40 or 50. For the beer connoisseur, a fact to be noted is that Mark has had his mains water analysed and compared to the original well in the brewery and now by re-hardening the water recreates the original style of beer which was brewed in the area. "Many people try to imitate Burton style beers but we would rather get back to what has always been brewed here. So our Rebellion IPA really does bring brewing back to Marlow". The name Rebellion was chosen to conjure up an image of Marlow's past (a Parliamentarian stronghold in the Civil Wars) plus the feeling that it is time for people to make a stand against the relentless levelling out of taste by national brewers.

The beer is:

Rebellion IPA	1038/39°

REEPHAM BREWERY

1 Collers Way, Reepham, Norfolk, NR10 4SW. Tel: 0603 871091

When Ted Willems left university twenty years ago, he wanted to be a chemical engineer. Unfortunately, the world of chemical engineering had nothing to offer him, so the world of brewing gained a valuable recruit. Ted started at one of the biggest breweries by helping manage the building of the Mortlake Brewery in London and has slowly worked down in size until he arrived in Reepham in Norfolk.

It had long been his ambition to set up a small brewery in Norfolk and his first attempt was with the owners of the Star

Brewery in Norwich, a brewpub which quickly sank without trace. Nothing daunted, Ted moved on to Reepham, not too far from his original hometown of Great Yarmouth, and started up his brewery in 1983. He has been there ever since. Other small breweries had come and gone locally, but Ted reckoned that with his management experience from a big brewery environment (and the enthusiastic support of his parents) he could make a go of it. History has proved him right. Nowadays his parents are still involved (sometimes even helping with deliveries) and the business thrives.

But here's a little tip for visitors. Proud as Ted is of his brewery, if you really want to make him happy, ask him about his local bowls team (he modestly hints that he has been referred to as the 'star player'). His only regret with the team is that the pub they used to play behind has gone, leaving the green, but no refreshments!

The beers are:

Granary Bitter	1038°
Dark	1040°
Velvet Stout	1043°
Gold	1044°
Rapier Pale Ale	1044°
Old Bircham Ale	1046°
Brewhouse Ale	1052°

REINDEER BREWERY

10 Dereham Road, Norwich, Norfolk, NR2 4AY. Tel: 0603 666821

Early in the 1980s when Wolf Witham and his partner at the time looked around for somewhere to start a brewpub, they really wanted to get out of Norfolk. Having looked all over England, they followed David Bruce's example of getting close to a large student population and found exactly the right spot on their own doorstep in Norwich. The Reindeer Brewery has a lot to thank David Bruce for – not only did they buy one of his brew plants, they later took on his Production Director, Colin

Summers who trained them in the early days and who has now returned to David Bruce as a Head Brewer.

'When we started', remembers Wolf, 'my partner then was an artist in brewing – his beer was so good that we sold out the first 15 barrels in four days! Later he wanted to leave the business, because it was just too hectic and my current partner, Andy Howard joined me.' Since the early days they have doubled the size of both the pub and the brewery (and now have the longest bar in Norwich) and have had a succession of interesting beers available, including their Janet Street Porter, which displayed a set of set of teeth as a pump clip. They are probably the only brewery in the country who are a mascot for an RAF Squadron (the 42nd) for whom they have brewed a special 1042°. Wolf and Andy like to pride themselves on their building skills, although drilling straight through the main power cable once blew Andy across the room into the malt store. They are currently talking about buying more pubs, and more casks and selling into the free trade around the area. 'Drinkers used to think of brewpubs as quirky and brewing funny old beer.' says Wolf. 'I think we are teaching the people round here to regard us just a bit more seriously!'

The beers are:

Moild	1034°
Bevy	1037°
Gnu Bru	1042°
Bitter	1057°
Red Nose	1057°
Sanity Claus	1067°

RINGWOOD BREWERY LTD

138 Christchurch Road, Ringwood, Hants. BH24 3AP

Brewery buffs will know that Ringwood Brewery was started in the earliest days of the small independent brewers' renaissance by the legendary Peter Austin. They will also know that the brewery's most famous beer is Old Thumper, immortalised in

1988 at the Great British Beer Festival as the Supreme Champion Beer of Britain. But they probably don't know that the beer started as a favour to a friend with a brewpub who didn't have the brewing capacity to meet his own commitments and was named through a competition in the local paper. And they are also probably unaware that today's Managing Director David Welsh started life at the brewery as an unpaid part-time helper because he was 'obsessed with breweries'. Admittedly David very rapidly became a partner, abandoning a more conventional career as a shipbroker in the city to embrace the life of a brewer. (Apparently Peter Austin thought that his city experience had made him a whizz at finance – David claims that he was mistaken, although the brewery has become so successful, there must have been some basis for the idea!)

Nowadays, there is no doubt that Ringwood is probably bigger than most small independents, and with a staff of 20 (including brother Nigel Welsh) they have a comparatively giant payroll (but including staff who run the brewery shop). Just the same as their smaller brethren, they do like a bit of fun – why else would they have transported their entire staff to the French town of Pont Audemer a couple of years ago to take part in a pedal car race! And why did Peter Austin start the brewery in Hampshire in the first place? Apparently he left the Hull Brewery after retiring as head brewer and came down to Hampshire to take up sea-fishing, only apparently (and embarrassingly) there were no fish on that stretch of the coast. So he took up brewery building instead (starting with Monty Python's Terry Jones brewplant – see Summerskills Brewery as well) and the rest is history . . .

The beers are:

Ringwood Best Bitter	1039°
Fortyniner	1049°
Old Thumper	1060°
Porter	1046°/1048°

RISING SUN INN

Knowle Bank Road, Shraley Brook, Audley, Stoke-on-Trent, Staffs. ST7 8DS.
Tel: 0782 720600

Sam Hollins had always enjoyed a jar or two at the Rising Sun, just up the road from his farm near Stoke-on-Trent. So when the old landlord let it be known that he was thinking of retiring, Sam though it would be an easier way of life than that of a farmer. How wrong he was! When he and his wife Gill looked through the deeds of the 200 year-old pub they discovered that beer had been brewed there in the last century, and so Sam decided he would like to revive the tradition.

In June 1989, after getting a brewplant from another pub, they set up to produce their four beers. From never having brewed before in his life, Sam's beer now boasts many faithful fans. He has recently taken to bottling some of his strongest brews, but it rarely sees the outside world because it is snapped up so quickly by local beer enthusiasts. Of course Sam misses his cattle which he used to raise on his farm but he tries to keep his hand in with livestock with his children's riding ponies on the small piece of land they have retained. As well as the ponies and the horses, he also regularly welcomes bikers to camp behind the pub and will soon be able to let rooms to visitors. For those who can't stay however, Sam runs a bus service which provides transport for parties of doctors, police and other local groups. As he says, he brings them in, gives them lots of his beer to drink and then takes them home again!

The beers are:

Rising Sun	1040°
Setting Sun	1045°
Sun Stroke	1056°
Total Eclipse	1072°

ROOSTERS

Unit 20, Claro Business Park, Claro Road, Harrogate, Yorks, HG1 4BA. Tel: 0423 561861

It was 1992 when Sean Franklin started up his second brewery. He gave up the first one because he got bored with the man who owned the barn in which it was housed, putting up the rent every time Sean appeared to getting more successful. That was five years ago, and Sean initially filled in his time as a taxi-driver, but the lure of the yeast eventually got the better of him and he simply had to go back into brewing. He now brews around 16 barrels per week in a business park unit and has succeeded in making some headway in the conurbations around Huddersfield and Halifax, with new markets

opening up all the time. But why did he start originally? He had always been in the wine trade, and in common with many other small brewers he was encouraged to look into brewing because of the success of other businesses. Not one to be unprepared, Sean taught himself to brew the hard way, getting through some forty home-brew attempts before he was satisfied with the result. The name Roosters is an interesting one, having been chosen because the cartoon rooster, which serves as the brewery's emblem is a cheerful bird, which does not take itself too seriously, which Sean thinks is very important when talking about ale: 'Too many people have forgotten that beer is a social drink, to enjoy with your friends and to be drunk for pleasure rather than as an academic tasting exercise. The Rooster stands for someone who won't fit into any pigeon holes, and I think that's me!'

The beers are:

Roosters	4.7%
Yankee	4.3%
Special	3.9%

ROYAL CLARENCE HOTEL

Royal Clarence Hotel, Esplanade, Burnham-on-Sea, Somerset, TA8 1BQ.
Tel: 0278 783138.

When Paul Davey first bought the Royal Clarence in Burnham on Sea, he knew that the small brewery attached would be an asset to the business. A chef by profession, Paul was intending to develop the culinary side of his new business while keeping the brewery running. What he didn't realise was that the brewery would grow to the extent that it has so that it dominates the business. Ten years ago, the brewery was producing enough to keep the customers of this seaside hotel happy, but now satisfies tastes much further afield.

The popularity of the beer can perhaps be demonstrated by their new head brewer who joined during 1993. Formerly Chairman of the Somerset CAMRA branch, Graham Dunbavan resigned from both engineering and his chairmanship to start brewing full time for Paul. Both he and Paul are steam train enthusiasts and they are delighted that a nearby station buffet at Yeovil Junction has become a regular outlet for their brews which as they point out saves time for local train-spotters and Royal Clarence beer fans.

Other local pubs are also increasingly enjoying Royal Clarence beer, while one pub asked them to brew a special celebratory ale as their 500th guest beer. The quality of what they produce perhaps explains why they regularly entertain groups of beer enthusiasts from all over the country as hotel guests. "It's good business", says Paul. "They don't have to worry about how to get home after they have been enjoying our hospitality!" Their beer is increasingly enjoyed further and further inland, and they currently produce 20 barrels per week. They are in the throes of moving the brewery to another site where they are able to brew sixty barrels per week, to satisfy the growing demand.

The beers are:

Clarence Pride	1036°
Pitchfork	1043°
Old Slug Porter	1045°
Regent	1050°
Firebox	1060°

RUDGATE BREWERY

Unit 2, Centre Park, Marston Business Park, Rudgate, Tockwith, N. Yorks.
Tel: 0423 358382

Bernard Lynley at Rudgate has done things the wrong way round. Many brewers buy pubs and become publicans, and many publicans start to brew their own beer while still in the pub trade, but very few give up their licenses to go in for full time brewing. Bernard claims that this gives him some insight into landlords' problems and he has a good idea of what time to ring them so that they are not too busy to speak to him.

In 1982, Bernard could see that the small independent brewers were starting to make a come-back. So he took a big step and went to David Bruce, who founded the Firkin chain, and learnt how to make his own beer. Eventually he left the pub trade to join what was then Big End brewery and finally set up on his own brewery on the edge of York. His partner Graham Ewbank arrived in 1993 and has spent a considerable amount of this time commuting from his home in Basingstoke.

Graham, formerly employed as a brewer by a large national company, was made redundant and has come 'back to his roots'. Bernard has some interesting theories about brewing. First, he claims it is not a job – because you need to really enjoy it to put up with the hard work and the dreadful hours; secondly, you need to sing to the beer as it ferments. 'Tell Laura I love her' is one of his own brew's special favourites. Thirdly, he claims, a brewer's wife (or husband) must be particularly understanding about the hours and the exhausting nature of the business. 'My wife Marlene is wonderful', he says. 'I have been known to help new brewers out and end up spending 24 hours in their brewery – and she still understands!' The brewery turns out around 15 barrels per week and the beers are named after York's historic connection with the Viking invaders.

The beers are:

Viking Bitter	1039°
Battleaxe Bitter	1044°

SHACKLEFORD BREWERY COMPANY

The Cyder House Inn, Peperharrow Lane, Nr Godalming, Surrey, GU8 6AN.
Tel: 0483 810360

When Ted Gibbs left the police force at a relatively early age, he needed something which would provide him with a living. Deciding to put the decision off, he went for a tour round Europe that was supposed to take a year, ran out of money in three months and needing some quick cash, took a job as a part time barman in a Surrey pub. Fortunately, the pub he worked in happened to be particularly well-run so he learnt a lot about working behind a bar very quickly and graduated to taking charge of another local pub's complete bar operation within about six months. After a few years he had learnt enough (he thought) to set up on his own, so he bought The Cyder House Inn, whose only asset was its cheapness. That was a few years ago, and since then the pub has become well-known and popular for people wanting a nice country pub for a good meal and good beer. Ted, who describes himself as 'lazy', developed the business so that he could employ enough staff to free him from too many day to day worries. And then he got bored. So he decided to put in a brewery despite knowing very little about brewing. But he learnt – so that now the 15 barrels per week he brews is sufficiently popular to sell out immediately, although he is still 'playing around' with recipes, and developing his skills even further. Ted has decided that he will not brew for 'the trade' so that his beer is genuinely only available either in his own pub or if you are lucky at a local fete or festival.

The beer that is regularly available is:

Piston Broke	4%	named after Ted's state immediately after brewing it

Other beers which are variously on offer are:

Old Shackle	4.8%	named after a local stream
Old Overdraft	1060°	

But don't rely on these being there when you want them because as Ted freely admits he brews what he feels like!

SNOWDONIA BREWING COMPANY

Gellilydan, Gwynedd LL41 4EH. Tel: 0766 85379, 0745 342423

There are very few breweries in Wales, and probably even fewer who can boast the sort of breathtaking outlook that brewery partners Martin Barry and Steve Talkington can enjoy at the Snowdonia Brewery. Located in the Bryn Arms pub in three acres in the middle of the Snowdonia National Park and overlooking the Moelwyn mountain range, it is truly beautiful, which is probably a relief to Steve who started life at the brewery commuting every weekend from his job as a publisher in London. Martin, on the other hand, had spent his whole working life in the catering business as a qualified chef. He fulfilled a boyhood ambition of owning his own business when he bought the pub.

The brewing started as a way of providing good priced beer for the pub and setting it apart from anything else around. Having originally learnt the techniques from Don Burgess at the Freeminer, they now brew as many as 10 barrels per week in their two-barrel plant – which means a lot of brewing! By now – hopefully – they will have moved into their new brewery in Penrhyn Deudraeth which will more than double their capacity. Steve's career as a brewer really took off when he was put in touch with Martin, having previously failed to open a brewery because of disagreements with the local water authority. He is planning to give up his London career very shortly to work full time at the brewery, concentrating on the sales and marketing side. The beer, however, does not prove difficult to sell, frequently winning top prizes at beer festivals (including overall Best Bitter at the Stockport Festival). They also accept commissions to brew specials including one which was a rice beer for a Himalayan Food Festival in Snowdonia. The Bryn Arms is also known locally as the home of particularly thriving pigs (who do well on the spent hops).

The beers are:

Mel-y-Moelwyn	1036/8°	3.7%
Snowdon	1051°	5%
Choir Porter	1045°	4.5%

SPRINGHEAD BREWERY

25 Main Street, Sutton-on-Trent, Newark, Notts, NG23 6PF.
Tel: 0636 821000

A former miner and British Telecom employee, Alan Gill had already decided what he wanted to do with the rest of his life when BT offered him redundancy. Other colleagues had bought pubs, but Alan had already proved that brewing was his forte. He had put together a very basic one barrel brewplant to test out the marketability of his own bitter, and was delighted to find that pubs were eager to take more than just an experimental barrel.

Of course, he should have known his beer would be popular, because as a member of the local Broadstone Morris Men, he had already test-marketed the beer among his fellow dancers (especially as they also form the backbone of the local CAMRA group). He calls them his 'quality control group' but it was because of their encouragement that he began brewing commercially. 'They kept saying that my beer was as good as what they bought in pubs, so I decided to give it a try'. One year later, the brewery is producing seven or eight barrels per week, and Alan has to think very hard now about expansion. Wife Yvonne is a key player in the business, having originally acted as his drayman, and children Erin, Ben and Joe are full of encouragement (especially when violinist Erin hears her father singing to his beer). They are a musical family, with Yvonne a folk violinist, and Alan no mean blues singer. Son Joe is a budding artist and a further son Ben is more interested in growing things at the moment (including a ferret and a pet snake).

The beer is:

Springhead Bitter	1040°

STEAMPACKET BREWERY

The Bendles, Racca Green, Knottingley, WF11 8AT. Tel: 0977 677266

After eight years in the Steampacket pub, Jim Mellor began brewing his own beer in 1991 with the intention of saving himself money. He really only wanted to have to avoid paying big brewers' 'silly prices' for beer and in an impulsive moment decided to do it himself. Very rapidly however the pursuit of excellence overtook the pursuit of economics and the quality of the beer became most important. What makes it even more pleasing for Jim is the fact that not only does he brew the beer himself, but he built the plant himself and has learnt the whole of the brewing process from scratch very rapidly. 'The people who started by brewing at home have an advantage', he claims. 'At least they had done it before. I had to learn as I went along!'

This policy seems to have worked because over the months more and more beer enthusiasts have been making their way to this 'small town pub'. The pub itself is rapidly becoming well-known in beer enthusiasts in West Yorkshire. Set beside a canal the pub also provides a watering hole for long boats (both tourists in the summer and year-round professional bargees with cargoes of oil and coal out of Hull). The fame of the beer is also spreading outside his own pub. He now brews around 30 barrels a week and he supplies a rapidly increasing number of outlets. With a capacity of some 90 barrels per week, there is plenty of scope for Jim to expand so look out for his cheekily named beers! (He has taken advantage of his surname to adopt a Lady Chatterley's Lover approach!)

The beers are:

Gamekeeper	1036°	
Chatterley	1037°	(a Weiss beer)
Bito Black	1040°	
Bargee	1048°	
Foxy	1039°	

STOCKS

The Holcross, 33-34 Hallgate, Doncaster, S. Yorks, DN1 3NL. Tel: 0302 328213

Stocks was originally started because Michael, the son of Managing Director David Jenkinson was interested in beer. Tragically, Michael died early in 1993, but the brewery, part of the large Cooplands firm of meat processers has become established as a thriving business in the centre of Doncaster. The company itself has been established some 62 years and the brewery has been going for eleven years.

This brewery must be one of the most substantial of the small independent breweries, being part of a large company which employs some 1100 people, but it retains the aims of all small independent brewers to maintain rigorous standards and provide a traditional venue for beer drinkers. David Jenkinson is proud of the brewery's adherence to the principles of only using pure ingredients for the beer with no additives. He is also proud of the brewery's fine record in winning prizes for their beers in festivals. The brewery and the Holcross pub occupy what was once a shop, made available when the Doncaster shopping centre moved further out of town. The site now houses a very traditional pub, along with a beer garden and of course the brewery which produces around 15 – 20 barrels per week. 'It's very open – people can walk through the garden (preferably by appointment) and get to the brewery to see for themselves how the beer is made', says David Jenkinson. The beer has established a name for itself in the surrounding area (maybe because of all those prizes!) and is available particularly in the North East in places such as Darlington, Durham etc.

The beers brewed are:

Stocks Best Bitter	1039°
Stocks Select Bitter	1044°
Old Horizontal	1054°
St Leger Festival Porter	5.0%

SUMMERSKILLS BREWERY

Unit 15 Pomphlett Farm Industrial Estate, Broxton Drive, Billacombe, Plymouth, PL9 7BG. Tel: 0752 481283

The total expertise of Summerskills partners alcohol production experience originally consisted of one home wine kit. But Carl Beeson and Rick Wilson maintained that years of consumption gave them an insight into what the customer really wanted. Rick had been a hotelier and a chef by profession and was about to sell his hotel. Carl after many years in the Royal Navy had been on land for about sixteen years and had recently been made redundant from his job as a director of a food company.

Together, they decided to set up a brewery and eventually bought Monty Python star Terry Jones' old brew plant and set about brewing (this brewplant does seem to have done the rounds – see Ringwood Brewery) from Adam Summerskill. At first this was not arduous; they had no customers and could brew about once every seven weeks to satisfy the meagre demand. Nowadays however they have to brew two or three times per week and find that everything they produce has a ready customer. This is perhaps some explanation of how they became the runners up in the Radio Times Radio 4 Enterprise Award in 1992. When questioned they claim nothing interesting ever happens in the brewery. Perhaps I should have spoken to some of the pubs where they deliver their beer. For instance 'Biltong', the ex-South African paratrooper landlord at Wilderbeest Hall (otherwise known as the Thistle Park Tavern in Plymouth) is regaled by Carl and Rick with South African songs as he takes delivery of his beer. Earlier this year they also did a special one-off Archers Radio Programme brew of 'Shires'.

The beers are:

Summerskills Best Bitter	1042°
Whistle Belly Vengeance	1046°
Ninja Beer	1049°

THOMAS MCGUINNESS BREWING COMPANY

Cask & Feather, 1 Oldham Road, Rochdale, Lancs, OL16 1UA.
Tel: 0706 711476

Thomas McGuinness himself sadly died early in 1993, but his life-long friend and head brewer, Eric Hoare told me the following story of how the brewery was started:

'What makes a man give up a cushy job as a publican, with plenty of dosh rolling in, holidays abroad with his wife and family two or three times a year and a secure future to embark on a project in which he had no previous experience, which is shrouded in mystery and uncertainty and could cost a hell of a lot of money in the middle of a recession? Eccentric, stupid, all these things you might say. The key answer to all these questions is FRUSTRATION. Frustration at trying to negotiate a measly 3% discount off a barrel of beer from a big brewer. At this time Tom and I would go out of our way to find a pub that sold a good selection of cask-conditioned beers, and we noticed an increase in small independent breweries popping up all over the place. So Tom said to me: 'If they can do it, we can.'

The seed had been sown. But what of the many thousands of questions that had to be answered – like where the heck do you buy a brewery? Surely not at Kwiksave. How do you make beer anyway? Is it like brewing a cup of tea or coffee? We were soon able to learn the answers to many of these questions. As we had no previous experience in the art of brewing we decided to opt for a plant which would be easy to use and would give us many years of trouble-free brewing. The company we used suggested that we should have a Full Mash set up complete with our own mill; well it sounded posh enough so we said OK. They also said we would need three Fermenting Vessels – in fact four were installed. Why, I don't know. Perhaps it was "buy three get one free". Who cares, at least it enabled us to increase our capacity by an extra five barrels.

'This was great, a lovely stainless steel brewing plant, an instruction sheet just like a Teasmaid; fantastic, but where do you find an original recipe? Fear not, hidden in the vast corridors of what used to be Manchester Polytechnic hides a brewing wizard called Dr David Sheldon who appeared as our Fairy Godfather (and what a Fairy Godfather!) with a quick explanation of what colour, flavour and strength we wanted our beer to be like he popped up like magic with three perfect recipes of two bitters and a porter. But the story does not finish there. Tom's finishing touch was a granite plaque inscribed 'The Thomas McGuinness Brewing Company' which was installed over the Brewery door. 'Where's my name?', I asked. 'On your bike', said Tom, 'My brewery, my name.' But what he was most concerned about was beating the big brewers and he leaves no better epitaph than his own words: if you fancy doing it, DO IT!

The beers are:

Thomas McGuinness Bitter	1038°
Junction Bitter	1042°
Tommy Todd	1050°

TINTAGEL BREWERY

Min Pin Inn, Tregatta, Tintagel, Cornwall, PL34 0D. Tel: 0840 770241

Marie Hall is a brewer and dog breeder and with her daughter runs an all female brewery. Marie's other interest is her dogs, Miniature Pinchers, who feature on her inn sign and give her pub the name The Min Pin Inn – the sign shows a Min(iature Pincher) standing on a Pin (cask). Marie will tell you modestly that she has done 'fairly well' in her dog breeding career – in fact her animals have featured on the Pedigree Chum advertisements on TV and won a 'Best of Breed' class at Crufts several years ago. They are now in their ninth year in the pub, after a lifetime in the licensed trade. Marie is carrying on a long English tradition of female brewers (or brewsters as they are more correctly known) and she finds that she is well accepted in what has become a male dominated industry. 'But then most things are allowed in Cornwall'. The brew pub is one of the smallest in the country so the beer is rarely available outside its doors. 'However, we do sometimes suddenly decide to go into mass production' says Marie 'and you might just find our Brown Willy or Legend elsewhere'.

The beers are:

Legend Bitter	1035°
Brown Willy Bitter	1055°

TIPSY TOAD BREWERY

St Peter's Village, St Peter, Jersey, Channel Isles. Tel: 0534 485556

As natives of Jersey Steve Skinner and his wife Sarah thought that the vogue for pub breweries that was beginning to develop in London in the 1970s and '80s was just the thing for their homeland. The local brewers refused to make anything except keg bitter and very little cask-conditioned ale found its way onto the island from the mainland, so it was obvious that Steve could make his own.

Their first problem on trying to set up a brewpub like this was to find the premises. Most pubs were tied firmly to breweries and it was a brave move of the former owner of the Star to agree to sell it to Steve free of tie. Having found the pub premises, the next problem was the name. Bearing in mind traditional Channel island rivalries, Steve had at first thought of calling the brewery something based on 'Crapaud' the local term for frog (as the Guernsey people call the Jersey residents). Feeling that this could lead to some unfortunate mistakes, he opted instead to translate the word into English – Toad. Even the term'Tipsy' was frowned upon at first by the authorities as

they felt it would lead to inebriation by the local residents (Steve reckons they had never heard the description of Jersey as '80,000 alcoholics clinging to a rock') but eventually common sense won the day, and The Tipsy Toad Brewery was founded just over a year ago. They currently brew around 8 to 10 barrels per week, selling mainly in the Star but also in one other local pub and a few private bars (including the Hockey club). They are set to open a new branch in St Helier in the New Year and are expanding their staff accordingly. Going back to old traditions, they have just trained a woman (brewster) as their brewer and will be taking on another female brewer shortly.

The beers produced are:

Star Drooper	1060°
Horny Toad	1050°
Jimmy's Bittery	1040°
Agile Frog	1038°

TRAQUAIR HOUSE BREWERY

Traquair House, Innerleithen, Peebleshire, Border, EH44 6PW. Tel: 0896 830323

I don't know of many brewers who can claim royal blood in their veins, nor of any who can number among their customers those most romantic historical figures, Mary, Queen of Scots and Bonny Prince Charlie, but Catherine Maxwell-Stuart has this distinction. She runs the magnificent Traquair House in Scotland and with it, its brewery. The wing in which the brewery now

sits 'only dates from 1700', says Catherine, but there are records which show that beer has been brewed on the site many hundreds of years before that. This is perhaps not remarkable when you consider that the house itself is the oldest continuously inhabited building in Scotland (a pair of gates to the house last closed when Bonnie Prince Charlie left the grounds and they will not be opened until the Stuarts are again back on the English throne).

What is amazing is that the brewplant was lost for decades until Catherine's father unearthed the equipment hidden deep in a pile of junk in 1965. 'It's lucky it was hidden', says Catherine, 'otherwise the coppers would all have gone into the war effort!' When Catherine's father discovered the brewplant, all still intact, he decided to have a go at making some beer, and with the help of students from Heriot-Watt University, using an old traditional recipe they eventually produced some saleable beer. At least they thought it was saleable. Unfortunately, since it was before the popularity of 'real' ale had really developed, they found it impossible to sell even at only three shillings per bottle – 15p in new money! But they persevered and now the bottled beer sells all over the world. Some beers are produced to celebrate family occasions such as wedding anniversaries and 21st birthdays. The beer is all fermented in oak (they believe they are the only brewery in the UK who do this with their total production) but as a branch of one of the oldest noble families in the British Isles you would expect them to retain the best of the old ways!

The regular beers are:

Bear Ale	1050°
Traquair House Ale	1085°

TRING BREWERY

81- 82 Akeman St, Tring, Herts, HP23 6AF. Tel: 0442 890721

As an experienced 'end user', it was a logical step for Kerr Hill to take up brewing when his own job as an area sales manager for a hi-fi company disappeared. It was a chance remark from life-long friend Richard Shardlow which really clinched the idea. Richard, whose father and brother were both head brewers, designs and installs breweries all over the world, and having seen so many other people successfully start up brewing businesses, felt that it was time to try it for himself. Having the marketing expertise of Kerr now available, it seemed obvious they should go into partnership. Richard still travels the globe setting up breweries (he was helping the Russians brew lager in 1993) while Kerry controls the day to day affairs of the brewery.

Even in its first year, the brewery has been so successful that it seems there has been no time for amusing anecdotes. However, Kerr does recall the time he came into the brewery very late one night after an evening in the local pub to switch on the coppers for the next day's work and decided that it was hardly worth going home, so he slept on the malt sacks! The beers are all named after local routes, so there is Ridgeway bitter, at the moment along with the newly introduced Old Icknield Ale. The regular Christmas Ale celebrates the amalgamation of Kerry's old Regiment, the 17th Lancers with the 21st Lancers (the 17th was a Hertfordshire regiment). It is 7.2%.

The beers are:

Ridgeway Bitter	4.0%
Old Icknield Ale	4.8%
Death or Glory Ale	7.2%

THREE TUNS

Bishops Castle, Shropshire. Tel: 0588 638 797

Since the Three Tuns can claim to be one of the four original independent brew pubs in the country, with brewing records going back as far as 1642, it is hardly surprising that a little diversification has crept in to the business.

The pub, run by the Wood family, brews some 12 barrels per week, all of which is consumed on the premises. The Woods bought it some 12 years ago, when Mr Wood Senior retired from his poultry farm. It is reckoned that Mr Wood had been the pub's oldest and most faithful customer, so it was only right that he bought it! The current most active member of the family is Dominic Wood who left a career as a commercial horticulturist to help in the pub, and did the brewing from 1984 to 1986. His love of plants has not left him and three years ago, he began selling plants in the pub garden 'because it's all an added attraction'. At one point they used to sell their beer through other pubs, but this detracted from the important business of selling it inside the building so they have stopped that. One would think with a success like theirs they would want to keep the recipe of the brew to themselves, but they are a generous family. They sell home brew kits to their customers, which very closely approximate to the taste of the pub's beer. ('Not too close of course – we want them to come back and drink ours – but it's very good none the less!').

The pub also prides itself on the quality of its food, the interesting aspect of the building, which conservationists find very hard to date, and most particularly on their brewplant. They have a classic example of a late nineteenth century brewing tower which people flock from far and wide to see. 'We were using coal as part of the process until a few months ago', says Dominic, 'but we have been forced to change to oil, which is less traditional but probably more convenient'

The beers are:

Light Mild	1035°
XXX Bitter	1042°
Steamer	1045°
Old Scrooge	1055°
Jim Wood's	1058°

TITANIC BREWERY

Unit G, Harvey Works, Lingard St., Burslem, Stoke-on-Trent.
Tel: 0782 823447

Perhaps naming your brewery after the most spectacular failure in British maritime history was not a good idea, but since Keith and David Mott bought out the original owner in 1988 (admittedly after he went into receivership) they have gone from strength to strength. Keith had been working for the business practically since he left school in 1986 and when he realised that the receivers were about to sell off the brewery for 'a song' he quickly stepped in to take advantage of their ignorance. They remained in their original premises for several years until the council started to increase the rents beyond what Keith and David considered sensible and they then moved to their current premises where they have 'four times the space for the same money'. They currently have the capacity to produce between 35 and 42 barrels per week and have grown steadily since the buy-out. David now runs a separate leisure shop and so is not involved in the brewery, but Phil Salt, the original head brewer is still there. They enjoy regular success at the local West Midlands Beer Festival. They do sound very sensible don't they? However, Keith does admit to a weakness for 'merry' marketing meetings, where the best names for the beers are conjured up and the brewery's usual ban on consumption of alcohol during working hours flies out of the window. At the time of going to press they were still trying to name their stout (the original name having fallen foul of another, rather larger, nearby brewery). Obviously another session round the marketing table was required. They have also recently acquired a pub in Stoke.

The beers are:

Best Bitter	1036°	
Lifeboat	1040°	
Premium	1042°	
Captain Smith	1050°	Named after the captain of the Titanic, one of Stoke's most memorable sons.
Anniversary	1050°	Brewed every 12th April, the anniversary of the sinking of the Titanic
Stout	1046°	

ULEY BREWERY

The Old Brewery, Dursley, Gloucestershire, GL11 5TB.
Tel: 0453 860120

For many years Chas Wright acted as a wholesaler for breweries all over the country. He was even the man responsible for bringing Theakston's to the South of England. Everyday, as he went about his business in Dursley in Gloucestershire he would pass the building next door, the now abandoned Prices Brewery, which had been built in 1833, as was proudly carved over a window in the brewhouse. Then, one day in 1984, the man who owned the building announced that he was planning to turn the premises into workshops. This did seem a shame, so Chas persuaded him that it would be much better to return it to its former function as a brewery. The owner was won over to his neighbour's arguments, and immediately Chas started building the brewery himself (literally).

The building had been empty for many years, so there was plenty of work to do. The winter months of 1984 were spent digging holes and building walls, building the brewplant at home or using a friend's fabrication workshop until the day in 1985 when the first brew was ready. The beer was a success. A beer which was brewed in his start up year for the Froster Beer Festival, a local event which raises vast sums for charity, proved so popular that when he took some of the same to the Great Western Beer Festival, it won first prize. This was an amazing achievement in any brewery's first year!

Whether the success of the beer had anything to do with the fact the brewery still uses its own original spring water I don't know, but the business has certainly thrived. The brewery now produces around 60 barrels per week, which as you can imagine, provides plenty of spent hops to dispose of. Chas has an interesting way of recycling this nutritious animal food, which also provides him with names for his beer. He has an arrangement with a friend who keeps a farm, who takes his spent grains to feed to the pigs and

cattle. As well as providing a profitable sideline for the brewery, it also gives inspiration for the names of the beer.

The beers are:

Uley Bitter	1040°	
Old Spot Ale	1050°	named after the Gloucester Old Spot pigs
Pigs Ear	1050°	
Pigor Mortis	1058°	

WILLY'S LTD

17 High Cliff Road, Cleethorpes, S. Humberside, DN55 8RQ.
Tel: 0472 602145

Willy's started off in a most unlikely way. It was originally a wine bar, opened and run by Bill Parkinson on the sea-front at Cleethorpes. Bill very astutely saw that beer was going to be an important part of his business – and he was the first pub in Cleethorpes to start taking guest ales. But it had taken him some time to get a license for draught beer. Eventually he had to go all the way to Crown Court to get permission to put in hand pumps. Meanwhile, it was obvious that it was not going to be easy to buy the beer in as a completely free house. He was forced to buy the beer initially from a local off-licence who sold draught ale over the counter and the nearest local brewery was Bateman's in Lincolnshire. However, as his range of ales expanded it seemed the obvious step was to start to brew his own. This was also due to be a long and arduous struggle. The premises next door to the Willy's became available, supposedly for 'quick sale' but it took 18 months before he gained possession. Bill had initially obtained quotations for a brewery in his original pub, but with all the extra space it was obvious that he had room for a much bigger plant, so he had to get some new quotations.

Eventually, in 1989, three years after the original idea for a brewery came to him, Bill was the proud owner of his very own.

As he says himself: 'It started because I had always been interested in microbiology (I even took a course in it purely as a hobby) and brewing was a logical way of combining business and pleasure, but I never realised how much hard work it was!' Bill is very proud of his brewery, which can be seen from the road through a glass panel, and he has also acquired another pub in nearby Grimsby where he sells his beers. They are also available elsewhere in the country. The plant produces around 15 barrels per week.

The beers are:

Willy's Original Bitter	1038°	
Mariners Gold	1042°	(can be found as Burkham Bitter elsewhere in the country)
Coxswain Special Bitter	1049°	
Old Groyne	1060°	(this is brewed with honey which gives it an unusual taste)

THE WOOD BREWERY LTD

Wistanstow, Craven Arms, Shropshire, SY7 8DG. Tel: 0588 672523

Just over thirteen years ago, the Wood family went into the brewery business. From such diverse backgrounds as poultry expert, chartered surveyor and retired businessman turned publican, they have since built up a thriving business. The brewery was started by Basil and son Anthony Wood. Another son, Edward, who now runs the brewery, only came in after six months to help out. Basil had already bought the village pub, the Plough, as a retirement business and it was Anthony, the Chartered Surveyor who persuaded him to set up the brewing side.

It was a steady but slow start; they had the pub as a guaranteed outlet and they had established several local customers. But it was when Ansells went on strike for six months in 1981 that their customer base exploded and they went from brewing 15 barrels a week to 50. This slowed down in the mid-80s and Anthony left to set up an estate agency leaving Edward in charge. Of course, over such a long time there have been many memorable moments, but perhaps the most notable was when the local RAF flew in a helicopter to pick up a firkin of their favourite beer for an imminent Royal visit. The crew stopped for lunch at the pub, strapped the firkin onto the spare seat and then flew off back in time for the beer to settle for the enjoyment of the visiting VIP.

The beers are:

Sam Powell Best Bitter:	1034°
Sam Powell Original Bitter	1038°
Parish Bitter	1040°
Severn Valley Railway Jubilee	1041°
Special Bitter	1043°
Sam Powell Old Sam	1048°
Wonderful	1050°
Christmas Cracker	1060°

WOODFORDE'S NORFOLK ALES

Broadland Brewery, Woodbastwick, Norwich, NR13 6SW. Tel: 0603 720353

What Ray Ashworth called 'a labour of love' began in the sixties when as a home brewer he started perfecting his technique. It came to full fruition a few years ago when Woodforde's Norfolk Nog was blessed with the title 'Champion Beer of Britain'. Ray's experience dates back before home-brewing kits were available. This was good training for commercial brewing. The quality of his beer, he says, cannot be put down to exceptionally tasty local water or the salty tang of the winds blowing off the North Sea – it's all to do with being a very good brewer and maintaining consistently high standards! He also says that his 19 years working for Barclays Bank gave him the financial expertise to run the business side of the brewery.

Ray set up shop after extensive research, initially with a part-time partner. The turning point came when he found someone to 'get out there and sell' his beer. At the same time as Ray developed the business side of his brewery, he found it necessary to move premises to keep up with his success. He has over the years moved from an anonymous industrial estate, to the stable block of a pub and finally to the present premises in agricultural buildings.

The 100 barrel-per-week brewery now resides amid the Norfolk countryside, and Ray's own 'nice clean smelly cows, magnificent British White Bulls and lots of calves who eat the brewers' grains'. The view from the brewery extends over thatched cottages, wide open fields and thatched country pubs. The nearest pub is the brewery tap, converted from the cottage next to the brewery. On the opening night of this 'new' pub, they ran out of beer. But, as Ray pointed out – 'Oh well, we didn't have to go far for emergency supplies!'

The Beers are:

Mardler's Mild	1036°
Norfolk IPA	1036°
Wherry Best Bitter	1039°
Norfolk Porter	1041°
Old Bram	1044°
Nelson's Revenge	1045°
Norfolk Nog	1049°
Baldric	1052°
Headcracker	1069°

WORLDHAM'S BREWERY

Smith's Farm, East Worldham, Alton, Hants, GU34 3AT. Tel: 0420 83383

Hugo Sharpe was no newcomer to brewing when he set up his Worldham brewery just over two years ago. He had already gained experience working with such diverse companies as Batemans and Truman's when he decided to go it alone. He could see the need for small independent brewers to add sparkle to the dull world of large breweries 'Things had got out of control with keg bitters – it was up to us brewers to add spice and character to what was already available to drinkers.

The brewery itself is housed in an old oast house, which is appropriate! Not many people realise that Hampshire still has a small hop production and it is Hugo's intention to make sure that at least a little of the hops that he uses are locally grown. 'The hop production in Hampshire is very limited, and it has to be said that Kent hops are very good, so there's every reason to use them – but we're a local beer, so a percentage of local produce is desirable.' The idea of 'local' is very important to Hugo. He sells his beer predominantly within a 25 mile radius of his brewery, mainly in the Guildford area because he believes that that's what local brewers are for. He produces around 20 barrels per week.

The beer is:

Old Dray Bitter	1042°

WYCHWOOD BREWERY COMPANY

Two Rivers Brewery, Station Lane, Witney, Oxon. OX8 6BH.
Tel: 0993 702574

Ten years ago, Paddy Glenny founded Glenny Brewery with Chris Moss as a partner. Now Chris Moss runs the brewery with his new partner, Ian Rogers. The story of this brewery has not been one of a meteoric rise to fame and fortune. As Chris says 'For years we plodded along at 22 to 23 barrels a week, lots of our pub customers went bankrupt and really the business was static. Then it took off. We had originally used the old maltings in Wychwood and we soon outgrew them and moved to a less attractive but more efficient unit on a factory estate. I'm pleased to say that we are bursting at the seams again now, since we now have eight pubs on lease stretching from West London to Bristol. We started off with one beer and now have four (five in the summer with Fiddlers Elbow).

The beers are:

Shires Bitter	1034°
Wychwood Best	1042°
Dr Thirsty's Draft	1050°
Hobgoblin	1058°
Fiddlers Elbow	

WYE VALLEY

69 St Owens St, Hereford, Herefordshire, HR1 2JQ. Tel: 0432 274968

In 1983 Peter Amor began brewing with David Mullings at the Abbey Brewery in Nottinghamshire. Eighteen months later partner David decided that he didn't want to be a brewer any more. Peter bought him out and moved the whole brewplant to outbuildings behind the Nag's Head pub in Hereford, renaming the brewery the Wye Valley Brewery. In 1987 they acquired a pub called the Barrels from Whitbread in Hereford, and began brewing behind it.

They're still there; Peter now employs three people, brews around 45 barrels a week and says 'We have quietly developed over the years and we like to be thought of as Herefordshire's brewery'. Peter gets quite enthusiastic about Herefordshire or 'the forgotten county' as he calls it, and is keen to point out that he only uses locally grown hops. 'Everybody always forgets that we are a big hop growing centre – now that Kent has cut back so much we might even have more hop fields than they do!' The brewery has grown over the years (the old plant which Peter replaced in 1992 now does service at the Freeminers Brewery in the Forest of Dean).

They sponsor their own quiz league – called the PHAT League, which Peter refused to explain. 'If you want to know what PHAT means you will have to come to Hereford to find out' he explained as he did his bit for promoting the county. Even the beers are named after the county of Hereford.

They are:

Hereford Bitter	1036°	
Hereford Pale Ale	1040°	
Hereford Supreme	1043°	
Brew 69	1055°	(Named after the address of The Barrels pub, Peter hastened to explain).

YATES BREWERY

Ghyll Farm, Westnewton, Aspatria, Carlisle, Cumbria. Tel: 06973 21081

When Peter Yates decided to cut loose from his job as head brewer at Jennings, he had to make his collection of goats and calves homeless. They were living in the barn next to his farmhouse on his smallholding in Cumbria and he needed the room to set up his own business. The animals had been a paying hobby, providing Peter and his wife Carol with free milk – but unfortunately not enough income to form the basis of a new career. The logical step was, of course, for Peter to start a brewery.

1986 saw the first Yates Bitter on the market and since then the Yates have produced an average of 25 barrels per week. Peter modestly admits to winning 'quite a few beer festivals'. And what about the animals? The goats are still around the place, providing the family with milk, but the calves have gone. They still pay their way, and a suggestion that Peter might consider combining his beer and his goats' cheese as a commercial proposition seemed to go down well. Perhaps we can look forward to that one for the future.

The beers are:

Yates Bitter	1035°
Premium	1048°
Best Cellar	1052°

The Highly Biased Pub Selection

Why do we need another Pub Guide?

Why indeed? You would think there were enough already. Curiously enough, however, no-one has ever asked the brewers to nominate their favourite hostelries. Chefs are asked to recommend restaurants, writers recommend books – surely the people who make the beer would be well qualified to judge a good pub when they visit one. So the pubs in this book have all come highly praised, for one reason or another by brewers.

For the same reason that this is a highly biased beer guide, I have included some highly biased reasons why these pubs are worth seeing. Some of them are in other beer guides, some are not. They all serve small independent brewers' beers, and they all serve it in good condition.

If you want to know which brewers recommended which pubs, you will have to guess – maybe if you read the biographies and the comments together you may be able to match them up. But that's up to you – all I can say is "Happy drinking"!

THE 'GOOD PUB' LIST

Albion, The, 1 Pedley Street, Crewe, Cheshire. Tel. 0270 256234: Well-kept guest beer in a town which lacks guest beers.

L'Auberge Divette, Jerbourg Road, St Martins, Guernsey. Tel. 38485: The real ale is always at its best. It has a real fire in the winter, and in the summer a beer garden with superb views over the islands

Barrels, 69 St Owen Street, Hereford. Tel. 0432 274 968: Noisy brash local, mixture of people from all walks of life, from ex-Mayor, and councillors to out of work electricians.

Beehive, The, Southborough, Nr Tunbridge Wells, Kent. Tel. 0892 524151: Old, tiny! Difficult to find but well worth the search. Loads of real ales.

Black Horse, Torrington, Devon. Tel. 0805 22121: Very olde worlde, in centre of an ancient town.

Blackwood Arms, Common Lane, Littlewood Common, Nr. Beaconsfield, Bucks. Tel. 0753 642169: Beer range varies with at least 25 different beers each week. Out in the sticks and difficult to find but very worth it when you do. Traditional country pub with large log fire, good food and probably the nicest landlord you will ever meet.

Blue Anchor, Teign Street, Teignmouth. Tel. 0626 772741: Seven beers to choose from. At least four SIBA ales. Friendly dockside pub, a chance to learn choice language in many foreign tongues.

Blue Ball, Triscombe, Nr Taunton, Somerset: Lovely thatched pub set in the Quantock Hills with terraced beer garden. The idyllic setting is sometimes shattered by huge quarry lorries passing – but don't let that put you off!

Blue Peter, Polperro, Cornwall. Tel 0503 72743: Last pub before you fall in the water. On the harbour, used by fishermen and tourists – lots of character. Changed hands last year but new people seem to be doing a fine job.

Bridge Inn, The, Exmouth Road, Topsham, Nr Exeter, Devon. Tel. 0392 873862: A very famous pub kept in the family for many generations. At least 16 ales to choose from at any one time. The building at the back was once a brewery. A friendly welcome awaits you.

British Union Hotel, The, St Lawrence, Jersey. Tel. 0534 861 070: Excellent local pub, good food served seven days a week, ideal for families. Beer served in first rate condition.

Brittania Inn, Alcombe, Devon: Sells the beer faster than the brewer who recommend the place can brew it!

Bunch of Grapes, Bradford-on-Avon, Wiltshire. Tel. 022 586 3877: Lovely old pub of character, good food too.

Butterleigh Inn, The, Butterleigh, Near Collumpton, Devon. Tel. 0884 855407: Sixteenth century. Bar food is superb. The spaniel Cassie, eats drayman's gloves. The landlord, Pat is regularly seen out shopping in his specially built "Postman Pat" van.

Captain Hotel, La Foise, St Martins, Guernsey. Tel. 8990: Plenty of character; the beer is always kept well, and is dispensed through a fascinatingly antique beer engine.

Carew Arms, Crowcombe, Somerset: This pub is almost totally unchanged since the 1920s and the Landlady is one of the longest serving publicans in the country. Set on the edge of the Quantocks, it is also the meeting place for many of the hunting fraternity. Ask to see the resident pigeon which lives in a hat.

Carpenters Arms, Metherell, Cornwall. Tel. 0579 50242: Good pub, lots of beers and ciders – more a restaurant that sells beer. Renowned for food.

Cartwheel, The, Whitsbury, Nr Fordingbridge, Hampshire. Tel. 07253 362: Lots of beers, lovely food.

Castle Arms, Snape, Bedale, North Yorkshire: Chocolate box image, wonderful for summer day out or winter warmer by the fire.

Chase Inn, Chase Road, Upper Cole, Hereford and Worcester. Tel. 0278 732695: Nestles in Malvern Hills, no juke box, only games like bar billiards. Beautiful food, traditional beers.

Cherub Inn, Higher Street, Dartmouth, Devon: A really quaint, lovely old pub. The oldest inhabited building in Dartmouth – with all the things you expect from an old building. Good beer and good restaurant.

Clifton Hotel, 35 Clifton Street, Plymouth, PL4 0JF. Tel. 0752 266563: Very good pub, big supporter of SIBA beers – always has a good selection.

Cobweb, Boscastle, Cornwall. Tel. 08405 278: Old wine warehouse opened up as pub. Run by "old Cornish boy" with a genuine accent – not a "foreigner". Real character pub for tourists and locals.

Courtyard Hotel, High Street, Wiveliscombe, Somerset. Tel. 0984 23737: The best drinking pub in the town of two breweries. Occasional functions in cosy cellar bar. Landlord tells the worst jokes in the county. The headquarters of the Wiveliscombe Liberation Front.

Cricketers, The, Ockley, Surrey. Tel. 0306 627205: Good little country pub on Stane Street. Not only is the food and beer very reasonably priced, but the flowers deserve an accolade. Fortunately they are in hanging baskets and not on hand-pumps!

Crown, The, Ollands Road, Reepham, Norfolk: Has a terrific atmosphere, particularly on the special evenings which licensees Trevor and Liz organise and provide free hot dogs.

Cuckoo, The, Hamptworth, Landford, Nr Romsey, Hampshire. Tel. 0794 39032: Unique, old school house, looks just like a cottage. Customers bring their instruments and play together.

Dartmoor Union, Fore Street, Holberton, Devon. Tel. 075 530 288: Primarily an eating house with excellent beer. Just celebrated its 200th anniversary as a pub – but the building has also seen service as a cider press and a workhouse.

Denbant Mill Inn, Haverford West, Dyfed. Tel. 0437 766569: Old water mill. The gearing goes up through the accommodation. Set in 7.5 acres of wild life reserve. Ring for directions – set down a dirt track, but well worth the effort. Extremely good for foreign food, particularly curries. Landlord is a real ale enthusiast

Derby Tupp, The, Sheffield Road, Whittington Moor, Chesterfield: Excellent food, many guest beers and a friendly atmosphere. A very basic pub that gets really busy. Parking is a bit awkward as it is situated on the main shopping road through Whittington Moor, but worth the effort.

Digby Tap, Cooks Lane, Sherbourne, Dorset. Tel. 0935 813148: Probably one of the first pubs to have guest beers – ever changing selection. Nice old fashioned pub.

Dolphin Hotel, The Barbican, Plymouth: Very basic dockside pub, but it's opposite the famous Captain Jasper's legendary late-night establishment, so it's worth a visit for that.

Double Locks, The, Marsh Barton, Exeter, Devon. Tel. 0392 56947. Don't drive anything wide to this pub. Access is over a very narrow bridge and along canal tow-path. Beer is (mostly) served by gravity from a multi-level stillage behind the bar. Original and excellent bar snacks. Eccentric pub

Eagle and Child, Church Road, Wharles, Nr Kirkham, Lancashire. Tel. 0772 690312: Thatched roof, beamed ceilings, open fires, and a treasure trove of antiques.

East End Arms, East End, Lyminton, Hants. Tel. 0590 652223: Unpretentious pub on the edge of the New Forest; good range of ales, mostly served straight from the cask.

Eccle Riggs Manor Hotel, (full on license), Foxfield Road, Broughton in Furness, Cumbria. Tel. 0229 716398: This pub is great because the food is fabulous and the facilities are second to none – indoor heated swimming pool, sauna, golf course.

Eddington Arms, 186 Ladies Lane, Hindley, Lancs. Tel. 0942 59229: Wide selection of real ales plus house real ale.

Elephants Nest, Mary Tavey, Devon: In the middle of nowhere and doesn't look like a pub from the outside more like the farmhouse it once was. Renowned in the area for real ale and real old-fashioned pub food. Lots of good fun.

Elsted Inn, Elsted Marsh, Nr Midhurst, W Sussex. Tel. 0730 813662: Good and varied selection of beers. Welcomes dogs and children; good food, good garden, summer barbecues, public bar and games – Mickey Mouse darts. Picture gallery behind in ex-Ballards brewery.

Engine and Tender, The, Broome, Craven Arms, Shropshire. Tel. 05887 275: The welcoming licensees provide a range of beers and good food in a traditional pub atmosphere. Also camping and caravanning available.

Evening Star, 55 Surrey Street, Brighton, East Sussex. Tel. 0273 326931: Nine real ales, always changing, one always a mild. Manager is aiming to sell every beer produced in the country and to date has had at least 500, mainly from large independent brewers. Regular blues music. A good drinking pub. Simple bar with basic decor with pictures based on trams. Very close to main rail station.

Falkland Arms, Great Tew, Nr. Chipping Norton, Oxon. Tel. 0608 83653: Justifiably famous pub which has to be visited. Dating back to the 16th century with flagstone floors, thatched roof and huge inglenook fireplace. A listed building. Has appeared on TV countless times, most recently in the BT shares adverts staring Mel Smith. Also a training ground for pub managers, the licensee only taking on people with no previous experience, so that they can be perfectly trained in how to run a traditional pub.

Fleur de Jardin, Kings Mills, Cotel, Guernsey. Tel. 57996: Real enthusiasm for the real ale and has a warm and pleasant atmosphere – a beer garden in the summer months.

Fountain Head, The, Branscombe, Devon. Tel. 0297 80359: No machines, no music, just good beer, good food, and plenty of local chatter. Heaves in summer, best enjoyed in the colder months.

Four Marys, High Street, Linlithgow, Scotland. Tel. 0506 842171: Mature person's pub with eight changing beers always available – chosen by CAMRA as best pub in area five years running!

Fox Inn, Corscombe, Dorchester, Dorset. Tel. 0935 891330: One of the best and most sympathetic restorations of an old village pub for miles around. Beer garden is on the other side of the road, and signs like "No chips, no microwave, bring your own ketchup" say volumes about the proprietors.

Gardeners Arms, 46 Cliff High Street, Lewes, East Sussex. Tel. 0273 474806: Eight real ales, always changing. Simple bar split into two sections, occasional live music, landlord is real ale fanatic. Tried to sample every beer at Olympia Great British Beer Festival.

Gardeners Arms, The, West Street, Sompting Village, East Sussex. Tel. 0273 35618: A village local with a friendly atmosphere.

Golden Rule, The, 30 Yeaman Place, Fountainbridge, Edindburgh. Tel. 031 229 3413: Dedicated to selling cask conditioned ales in peak condition through superb cellar management.

Good Knight Inn, Cheriton Bishop, Devon: Interesting collection of old armour. Good family room with kiddies' playground outside

Great Northern Inn, The, Ossington Road, Carlton on Trent, Newark, Notts: Excellent facilities for children, with an enormous conservatory joining the public bar, rather than a room too far away. Food is good.

Green Inn, The, Llangedwyn, Oswestry, Shropshire: Beautiful rural marches setting, on village green offering an excellent menu seven days per week, and terrific variety of ales, served by hosts Gary and Robin Greenham.

Griffin Hotel, Attleborough, Norfolk. Tel. 0953 452149: Pub-cum-small hotel. Bed and breakfast. Good food, good beer, very friendly atmosphere.

Guildford Arms, 1 West Register Street, Edinburgh. Tel. 031 556 4312: A perfectly restored city centre Victorian pub – selling a comprehensive range of Scottish beers – good food too!

Hare and Hounds, Henley Road, Marlow, Bucks: Young couple (Gavin and Helen Dick) run this pub and provide very good food – they took over a little while ago and have really improved things!

Hatch, The, Hatchlands Road, Redhill, Surrey. Tel. 0737 764593: Certainly the bluest pub in the country but what shade of blue? The Landlord wears Bermuda shorts so presumably it is Atlnatic blue! Look out for the splendid Victorian blue pictures. The beer is pretty good too as they have been long time supporters of small brewers, offering an oft-changing range. The very best cheese and onion sandwiches for miles around.

Hawkley Inn, The, Hawkley Liss, Hants. Tel. 0730 84205: Very difficult to find, so such a relief when you do! Excellent food in bar and restaurant, good blues/rock/country music Wednesdays. Free juke box. Landlady is quite "out to lunch".

Hole in the Wall, Vernon Road, Scarborough, North Yorkshire. Tel. 0723 373746: Old fashioned, built into rock above St Nicholas Cliff. Beer always excellent.

Hooden Horse Inns Ltd. – a small chain that deserves patronage. The pubs have wooden floors, dim lighting and excellent Italian-based menus.

Hooden Horse, The Street, Great Chart, Nr. Ashford, Kent. Tel. 0233 625904.

Another Hooden Horse, Rolvenden Village Layne, Nr. Tenterden, Kent. Tel. 0560 241637.

Grand Old Hooden Horse, High Street, Cranbrook, Kent. Tel. 0560 713460.

Hooden on the Hill, Silver Hill Road, Willesborough, Nr. Ashford, Kent. Tel. 0233 662226.

Hunters Lodge, Cornworthy, Totnes, Devon: A real Devon pub, notable for the locally popular card game "Yuka" which is played there.

Imperial, Ivybridge, Devon. Tel. 0752 892269: Good food pub. Big kiddies' play area

Johnsburn House, Johnsburn Road, Balerno, Edinburgh, EH14 7BB. Tel. 031 449 3847: Voted Scottish pub of the year, winner of awards, and has two hundred different ales available per year. Listed building, once owned by the man who introduced Robert Burns to Sir Walter Scott.

Jolly Farmer, Cookham Dean, Berks: A village owned pub – forty villagers clubbed together and bought the place when it came up for sale and have leased it to a young couple. Beautiful setting – regulars really take an interest!

Kings Arms, Stockland, Nr Honiton, Devon: Beautiful pub serving great food. Beer cellar is one floor above the bar, and the payphone is an old call box.

Lamb, The, Birdham Road, W. Wittering, Nr Chichester, W. Sussex. Tel. 0243 511105: Stocks only SIBA beers from four local breweries; very nice owners and staff. Pretty pub near beach and sailing.

Leeming Motel, Leeming, Leeming Bar, North Yorkshire: Excellent beer right on A1 – marvellous to have such a good beer at a motorway service station (not for the driver, of course).

Lincolnshire Poacher, The, Mansfield Road, Nottingham. Tel. 0602 411584: Probably the most well known pub in Nottingham. Great selection of beers, well kept and a good menu. Basic town pub gets masses of business but very friendly staff. Have regular folk evenings and brewery tastings.

Lion Hotel, Bridge St, Worksop, Nottinghamshire: 15th Century inn origin. 32 en suite bedrooms, character bar, bar meals, restaurant, large function room, chef de cuisine standard, three star rated.

Maltsters Arms, Tuckenhay, Nr Totnes, Devon: Riverside pub owned by TV cook Keith Floyd. Renamed Floyd's Inn.

Masons Arms, Masons Arms, Magdalene Street, Taunton, Devon: Town centre pub – where the landlord is really into cricket and will gladly talk about Somerset County Cricket team (but may not be there when there is match nearby). Full of cricketing memorabilia. Food includes "steaks on a stone".

Mountain Inn, Lutton, Devon. Tel. 075537 247: Landlord always takes SIBA members' beer, and a good place for dog enthusiasts. Landlord wins prizes for his gun dogs.

Nags Head, Pilkhill, Thirsk, North Yorkshire. Tel. 0845 56739: Excellent Beer, good tap room. Food superb but slightly upmarket in choice and price.

Neville's Cross Hotel, Neville's Cross, County Durham: good value for money, pleasant Irish landlord; good ale; does accommodation at good prices.

New Inn, Hambledon, Hampshire. Tel. 0705 632466: It's a dying breed – the traditional pub with excellent ale and no food!

New Inn, Waterley Bottom, North Nibley, Gloucestershire. Tel. 0453 543659: Not the easiest pub to find, several miles down a very narrow country lane which stops at the pub. Recently voted Pub of the Year for Gloucestershire and the whole of the South West by CAMRA. Seven real ales dispensed through a range of antique hand pumps. This pub has also won many awards for its beautiful garden.

Newhampton Inn, Riches St, Whitmore Reams, Wolverhampton, West Midlands. Tel. 0902 745773: A warm welcome and first class choice at this real ale enthusiast's haunt.

Nog Inn, Feniton, Nr Honiton, Devon. Tel. 0404 850210: Situated on a level crossing next to Feniton station, this must be one of the few pubs in the country where train-spotters can indulge in their hobby and a pint at the same time.

Normandy Arms, Blackawton, Devon: A nice pub, most notable for being the home of worm charming made famous by television programmes such as "That's Life". Takes place annually on May Bank holiday.

Old Albion, Crantock, Cornwall. Tel. 0637 830243: Old place near beach. Young licensee doing all the right things. Good food etc.

Old Brewery House, Market Place, Reepham, Norfolk. Tel. 0603 870881: Traditional market town hotel with lots of character. Called the "brewery"; visitors think the beer is brewed on the premises!

Old Harkers Arms, The, 1 Russell Street, Chester. Tel. 0244 344525: A welcome high class boozer close to the centre of Chester. If you can fight your way to the bar you are guaranteed a good pint from a very wide range. A dangerous pub, as inside you could be struck by the cast iron columns that support the ceiling, whilst outside a canal beckons.

Old Plough, Bere Ferrers, Devon. Tel. 0822 840358: Absolutely beautiful; sail up the river to it – there are moorings for boats. Seafood pub – also famous for Maggie's Monsters, gargantuan pies of every description. Also close to railway station.

Old Spot Inn, Hill Road, Dursley, Glos: The brewer recommending this pub says the landlord is a "sex maniac" but has provided no corroborative evidence, so perhaps it is better to rely on the sandwiches where the meat is thicker than the bread.

Old Station Inn, Hallatrow outside Bath. Tel. 0761 452228: Supporter of local breweries. Better known for eclectic collection of ornaments including the controls of a jet fighter, piles of encyclopaedias, phone boxes etc. Somewhere to go when you are bored!

Osborne Arms, High Street, Lane End, Nr High Wycombe, Bucks: Great atmosphere – a really friendly pub, with six members of the Twine family running it. A true free house. Very good food.

Phoenix, edge of St Paul's, Bristol: Small traditional ale house – but the landlord really cares about his beer.

Pig and Fiddle, 2 Saracen St., Bath, Avon. Tel. 0225 460868: Six real ales, its own surfing team and surfing championship. Landlord Tom Gill (and wife Carol) has phenomenal energy; holds triathlon events, jamming sessions. Outside terrace very popular in the summer (shorts should be worn).

Plough, The, Rusper, Surrey. Tel. 0293 87215: Enterprising free house where regulars are deluded into thinking it has a ghost. Could this be the result of too much beer or a beam too far? Terrific range of well kept beers.

Poltimore Arms, Yarde Down, Near South Molton, Devon. Tel. 0598 710381: If you want to get away from it all, this is the place, a wonderfully old fashioned pub in a remote corner of Exmoor. So remote they don't even have mains electric. A great place to sit and enjoy a pint while listening to the generator chugging away gently in the background.

Prince Albert, Newmarket Street, Stow-cum-Quy, Nr. Cambridge. By 1993 had had 700 different beers in under six years. Not the most picturesque of pubs, but very friendly and welcoming. Gets very busy during race days. Landlord is hardworking, friendly and an accomplished marathon runner!

Prince of Wales, Mill Road, Marlow, Bucks. Tel. 0628 482970: Very good at looking after beer. Very nice friendly staff, jolly, amusing landlord – a locals' pub in a very touristy area, where the staff find time to encourage local trade.

Prince of Wales, 5 St Nicholas Lane, Aberdeen. Tel. 0224 640597: Lovely, unspoilt old pub – long bar – goes on for ever! Good cellar – beers always in tip-top condition.

Pym Arms, Devonport: Good natured abuse from the landlady is par for the course. Also known locally as "Arfamo" (run by a team named Arthur and Maureen).

Queens Head, Parsonage Lane, Icklesham, Nr. Hastings, East Sussex. Tel. 0424 614552: Varied beer range. Situated with superb views – with its large windows is a lovely pub in the summer. Decor consists of farming implements, a bees' nest and a bust of Gandhi (!) Very friendly, but very busy.

Queens Head, Minehead, Somerset: A well modernised large pub worthy of mention for being the only decent traditional beer outlet in an otherwise desert of a seaside town.

Railway, The, Yorton, Nr Clive, Shrewsbury, Shropshire. Tel. 0939 28240: The atmosphere is all that one would look for in a pub. Good beer at cheap prices with an open fire and friendly licensees.

Reindeer Inn, Main Street, Hoveringham, Notts. Tel. 0602 663629: This is a small cottage style pub with a small restaurant. Food is spectacular and the service is such that you get attention at all times when eating. Ideal for romantic evenings. Good selection of beers and friendly atmosphere.

Ribs of Beef, Magdelen Street, Norwich. Tel. 0603 619517: Terrific choice of real ales, friendly bar staff and marvellous chalk drawings of one of the guest ales.

Rising Sun, Altamum, Launceston, Cornwall. Tel. 0566 86636: Famous for being the other pub in Daphne du Maurier's Jamaica Inn. Well run country pub with good food. Landlord has been there 15 years.

Rising Sun, Gunnislake, Devon. Tel. 0822 832201: New landlord. Lots of beers and ciders. Good food. It has become very popular very quickly.

Rock Inn, Waterrow, Wiveliscombe, Somerset: The corny sign on the door "Never mind the Dog" was never truer. The pub's slogan is "Only the abuse is free". Called the Rock because it's built into a cliff face, and the cellar is actually under an overhang.

Rock, The, Chiddingstone, Edembridge, Kent. Tel. 0892 870328: Good beer, good company, good reasonably priced food, comfortable atmosphere. A genuine country pub which makes you feel welcome, with wonderful service. Particularly recommended by the recommending brewer's dog.

Roseneath, 79 Arden Street, Gillingham, Kent. Tel. 0634 852553: Friendly back-street pub with large garden at rear. Main feature is "Golly", the only known Snakehound in existence (if you believe Tim behind the bar). Worth visiting if inly to make Golly's acquaintance. Each year has a very good beer festival, the entire proceeds of which go to charity.

Royal Oak, Ellerdine Heath, Telford, Shropshire. Tel. 0939 250300: Longstanding CAMRA members Barry and Rose dedicate themselves to supporting good beers from local small breweries and those further afield.

Royal Oak, Loswithiel, Bodmin. Tel. 872552: Accommodation, good restaurant – all home-made food. Public bar with seven or eight ales always available.

Royal Oak, Luxborough, Nr Minehead, Somerset: Sypathetically restored village pub in the heart of Exmoor National Park serving a good selection of cask beers. Folk music on Friday nights by resident band and guests.

Schooner Inn, 146 Albion St, Southwick, East Sussex. Tel. 0273 592252: This pub is on the A259 by Shoreham Harbour with a nice view over the yacht Marina.

Seymour Arms, Witham Friary, near Shepton Mallet, Somerset: Few pubs have serving hatch still – still fewer have such low prices. It's difficult to find, but you'll save the cost of the journey! Authentic turn of the century atmosphere.

Ship Inn, Wheat Lane, Lathom, Nr Ormskirk, Lancs. Tel. 0704 893117: Canalside good food pub.

Shurton Inn, Shurton, Nr Bridgwater, Somerset. Tel. 0278 732695: Overlooks Hinkley Point Nuclear Station, so a great place to go to recover from the (free) tours of the place. (The beer doesn't glow in the dark!).

Silverton Inn, Fore St, Silverton, Devon. Tel. 0392 860196: Good basic village local, posh restaurant upstairs, food all home cooked. The landlord is very fond of France.

Springer Spaniel, Treburley, Cornwall. Tel. 0579 370424: Called this because – yes, you guessed, the owner really likes dogs. Recently much improved, good food, good beer.

Station Buffet, Manningtree, Essex. British Rail Station. Tel. 0206 391114: You have to get onto the platform to get into the pub, but they will give you your pint in a plastic glass if you're actually catching a train. Very smart – reputed to be a favourite pub of Tottenham Hotspur and Plymouth Argyll football teams.

Strode Arms, Cranmore, Somerset Tel. 0749 88450: Home of Somerset Railway (Connected with Rev David Sheppard), fantastic food. (If you can find this one you're doing better than I am!).

Sun Inn, Corfton, Craven Arms, Salop. Tel. 058473 239: Working his way through The Good Beer Guide, this licensee always has a good selection of beers. An excellent bar menu in lovely surroundings completes the package.

Tap, The, London Road, North End, Portsmouth, Hampshire. Tel. 0705 699943: A great range of ales at very reasonable prices.

Thistle Park Tavern, 1 Sutton Road, Plymouth, PL4 8JB. Tel. 0752 667677: Run by an ex South African Paratrooper, good beer. Also known as "Wilderbeest Hall".

Three Stags Heads, Wardlow Mires, Derbyshire. Tel. 0298 872268: Set in the Peak Forest in the middle of nowhere. Basic stone floors, small, always with three cask ales, no keg or lager but a splendid range of unusual bottled beers. Has folk music most Friday nights, and considering its whereabouts, get absolutely packed. Excellent for the walking fraternity; people obviously travel for miles to get there.

Tom Cobley Tavern, Spreyton. Tel. 064723 314: Fringe of Dartmoor. Traditional, flag-stone floor. Regular curry nights – all home cooked food. Indoor barbeque for special occasions.

Tormakin Hotel, Glendevon, Nr Dollar, Scotland. Tel. 0259 781252: Excellent bar and restaurant food in warm country pub atmosphere.

Turnpike, The, High St, Bawtry, Nottinghamshire: Beer garden, luncheons and bar meals.

Two Clomes, Quintral, Newquay, Devon. Tel. 873485: Ancient building. Used to be a bakery – hence "two clomes" – clomes is a dialect word for oven and they're still there. Good food and very friendly.

Two Pigs, Pickwick, Corsham, Wiltshire. Tel. 0249 712515: Incredible number of real ales, sawdust, live music, made great by present owners after previously being closed down. Own identical 'piggy' pump clips.

Village, The, 33 Wilton Rd, Salisbury, Wilts. Tel. 0722 329707: Landlord Joe Morris as well as providing a selection of good beers also offers garlic and chilli pickles which should only be attempted by the brave of heart and asbestos of tongue.

Wellington Arms, Park Road, Freemantle, Southampton, Hampshire 0703 227356: Village pub in the heart of town. Interesting memorabilia.

White Hart, High Street, Hampton, Middx. Tel. 081 979 5352: Eight hand pumps, simple bar, very busy pub excellent food. Functions catered for in separate room. Unlike many pubs in the area it is completey free from any commitment to any large brewer, and concentrates on offering the customer a superb choice of real ales. Mentioned by Charles Dickens in *Oliver*

Twist. Keep an eye out for the two biggest dogs you have ever seen – but don't worry, they don't wander round in the bar!

White Hart, Trudoxhill, Frome, Somerset. Tel. 0373 836324: Landlord Adam Rimmer has an infinite knowledge of British Rail and all things to do with it; even has a pair of BR socks. Also represented by what may be the worst pub cricket team in England, although with the help of a few "ringers" managed to win a match last year. (This one sneaked in – may well have a strong connection with Ash Vine Brewery!)

White Hart Bar, Dartington Hall, Totnes, Devon: Bartok and Beer. Part of the Dartington Hall School, and worth visiting in the summer vacation when it becomes a music school. Sit in the 12th Century bar where you can hear Shakespeare recited in the amphitheatre or listen to a string quartet.

White Horse, Hedgerley Village, Bucks: A family run free house with an extremely good reputation in the area. Beer is drawn straight from the cask from a good range behind the bar.

White Horse, Stogumber, Taunton, Somerset: Good pub in pretty village where only 5 new houses have been built since the war. Landlord is a computer and electronics buff and the pub is one of the centres for Stogumber Festival which has featured many great musicians playing in the church opposite, including Van Morrison.

White Horse, 25 Townfield Street, Chelmsford, Essex CM1 1QJ. Tel. 0245 269556. Splendid pub.

White Horse, Castle Street, Hertford. Tel. 0992 550127: This small pub stocks a wide range of ales in excellent condition and has a convivial atmosphere.

White Horse, Thruxton, Hampshire. Tel. 026 477 2401: Very old pub, closed down for a road to be built almost over the top. The present owner brought it back after the road was finished.

White Swan, 45 Baptist End Road, Netherton, Warwickshire. Tel. 0384 256101: Good selection of changing guest beers.

Wild Goose Inn, Combeinteignhead, Devon. Tel. 0626 872241: Lots of antique furniture, quiz nights, landlord very keen on jazz and has jazz nights on Mondays.

William IV, The, Little Common Lane, Bletchingley, Surrey. Tel. 0883 743278: Recently tastefully redecorated in pink and green, but do not mention this to the Landlord and Lady who are convinced the pub is oyster and viridian or some other exotic colours! The food is excellent quality and value – the lunchtime specials are exceptional. Do not worry if, after a few pints, you leave and find that you are sloping – you're in the beer garden. Geoffrey the dog is omnipresent.

William IV, The, Little London, nr. Shere, Surrey. Tel. 0483 202685: A beautiful pink pub almost impossible to find, but well worth the walk! This is a typical example of a pub that has thrived in private hands when loosed from the iron grip of a national brewery. The food is renowned, and in winter game caught by the Landlord is on the menu. If you are fortunate they might have a pig roasting over their open fire.

Woolpack Inn, Slad, Stroud, Glos: Unspoilt country pub noted for magnificent conversation "and grunts" in public bar. The haunt of Martin the Diesel and the much better known Laurie Lee, poet and author of Cider with Rosie.

Wych Way Inn, Par, Cornwall. Tel. 0726815601: Big relatively modern pub; run by Essex family who have improved the pub no end; excellent chef , so good food (excellent for weddings or celebrations) – even a good car park.

Wyndham Arms, Kingsbury Episcopi, Martock, Somerset: One of the best examples of a true community pub. Even the play-group meet here and the pub itself is a magnificent example of how a pub should be run and deservedly well supported by locals and visitors alike.

SIBA and Beer Lovers

The following are pubs which have sworn allegiance to the Small Independent Brewers Association by actually joining *The Beer Lovers Club* and so help spread the word about the huge variety of small independent brewers' beers.

Crown Hotel, High Street, Bildeston, Suffolk

Inn on the Green, Watton Road, Datchworth, Herts

Lord Hill Inn, Main Road, Ketley Bank, Telford, TJ2 ODH

Lytton Arms, Park Lane, Knebworth, Herts

Railway Inn, Station Road, Newnham-on-Severn

Red Lion, West Dean, Wiltshire.

Rosary Tavern, 95 Rosary Road, Norwich, Norfolk

Ship Inn, 94 Furnham Road, Chard, Somerset

Shoulder of Mutton, New Road, Mytholmroyd, Halifax, West Yorkshire

Station, 2 Warrington Street, Ashton-under-Lyne, Lancashire

Three Guns, North Wootton, Sherbourne, Dorset

Tynllidart Arms, Capel Bangor, Aberystwyth, Dyfed

Wheatsheaf Inn, Marsh Green, Edenbridge, Kent

The 'Where to Find the Breweries' Index

This index lists the towns and counties in which the breweries in the second section of this book are located. To find the pubs that sell the beers, please look in the following index.

Y

The 'Where to Find the Pubs that sell the Beer' Index

This index lists the towns and counties in which the pubs in the third section of this book are located. To find the breweries that brew the beers, please look in the preceding index.

HAVE A HALF ON US!

With this voucher (photocopies not valid) you can enjoy one year's HALF-PRICE membership of
THE BEER LOVERS CLUB.

For just £5.00 (normal price £10.00) you can enjoy six *Small Beer* newsletters containing:

The latest news about the oldest and newest SIBA breweries – hear about the new breweries **as they open.**
Sixteen free half-pint vouchers for beer in pubs all round the country.
Special offers from SIBA brewers (including 10% off take-home polypins from SIBA brewers).
Special concessions at SIBA Beer Festivals.
Competitions.

Cheques should be payable to:

The Small Independent Brewers Association

and sent to:

The Beer Lovers Club
9 Windsor Road
Finchley, N3 3SN

Name: ....
Address: ....
....
....
....